QUAKER® OATS

FAVORITE RECIPE COLLECTION

Library of Congress Cataloging-in-Publication Data

Quaker Oats favorite recipe collection.
     p.   cm.
   Includes index.
   ISBN 0-7835-4863-X
   1. Cookery. 2. Brand name products.
I. Quaker Oats Company. II. Time-Life Books.
TX 714.Q35 1996
641.5—dc20   96–32916
                         CIP

TIME® LIFE BOOKS

The Quaker Oats Company

Recipe Development
The Quaker® Oatmeal Kitchens

Photographers
Jim Wheeler, Mary Baber, Kathy Sanders,
Peter Barry, Pam Haller, Deborah VanKirk

Food Stylists
Mary-Helen Steindler, Gail O'Donnell, Judy Vance,
Lois Hlavac, Helen Burdett, Lynn Gagne

Prop Stylists
Nancy Wall Hopkins, Wendy Marx, Karen Johnson,
Renee Miller

Copy Writing/Editorial Direction
McDowell & Piasecki Food Communications, Inc.

First printing. Printed in U.S.A.

Time-Life Custom Publishing

Vice President and Publisher
Terry Newell

Director of New Business Development
Phyllis Gardner

Director of Marketing
Rebecca C. Wheeler

Sales Associate
Wendy Blythe

Managing Editor
Donia Ann Steele

Editorial Director
Jennifer Pearce

Program Manager
Trish Palini

Design
Studio A

Production Manager
Carolyn Bounds

Quality Assurance Manager
Miriam Newton

Pictured on title page (clockwise from top left): *Easy Apple Custard Pie, Lemon Blueberry Oatmeal Muffins, Fresh Fruit Crisp, Go Bananas Cookie Sundaes, Peach Muesli With Berries, Peanutty Crisscrosses.*

Pictured on contents page (top to bottom): *Sunday Supper Meatloaf, Honey Lime Oat Muffins, Oatmeal Butter Brittle Cookies.*

QUAKER® OATS
FAVORITE RECIPE COLLECTION

WHO IS
THAT MAN?

The "figure of a man in Quaker garb" on the Quaker® Oats package was the first registered trademark for a breakfast cereal (1877). One of the founders of The Quaker Oats Company, Henry Seymour, selected this symbol to represent virtue and give consumers confidence in Quaker Oats.

When you see the smiling man on the Quaker® Oats package, you're likely to remember steaming bowls of cereal and fresh-from-the-oven oatmeal cookies and with good reason. For 120 years, Quaker Oats has been America's favorite hot cereal, and since the 1890s, it also has been a popular baking ingredient. In fact, the Quaker Oats package was the very first package to have a recipe printed on it–an oatmeal cookie!

Although the recipes on the package have changed over the years, the great taste and wholesomeness of Quaker Oats has remained the same. Quaker Oats is a whole grain, which means it contains the original bran, germ and endosperm. Nothing has been added or taken away so that you will enjoy all of the flavor and nutrition that grows naturally in oats. Whole grain oats are a good source of iron, thiamin, phosphorus and magnesium. And both Old Fashioned and Quick Quaker Oats are low in fat, sodium free, cholesterol free and preservative free.

THE FIRST OATMEAL COOKIE

In 1908, Oat Cakes became the first oatmeal cookie to appear on the Quaker® Oats package and the first-ever recipe to appear on a cereal package in the United States. During the next 85 years, oatmeal cookies changed as America changed, and the original Oat Cakes were followed on-package by:

Quaker Oats Macaroons (1930)*
Crisp Oatmeal Cookies (1935)
Mary Alden's Favorite Oatmeal Cookies (1943)
Famous Oatmeal Cookies (1955)*
Quaker's Best Oatmeal Cookies (1987)*
Chewy Choc-Oat-Chip™ Cookies (1992)*
Vanishing Oatmeal Raisin Cookies (1994).

*Featured in this book.

In addition to adding whole grain goodness to all kinds of recipes–from cookies and muffins to meatloaf and pizza crust–versatile oats impart a delicious nutty flavor and chewy texture. It's Quaker Oats' wholesomeness and taste that have made it a pantry staple in millions of kitchens.

The recipes selected for this 120th anniversary treasury were developed in The Quaker Oatmeal Kitchens, a trusted source of recipes for generations of American cooks, or were winners in our annual recipe contest. Whether you've been cooking and baking for years, or just beginning to explore the kitchen, you'll love this book. The directions for all of the recipes are numbered so they're easy to follow, and step-by-step illustrations make techniques like kneading dough simple. The main dish recipes include preparation and cooking times, and there are helpful tips in every chapter.

RECIPE SYMBOLS

♥ Lower Fat
All of these recipes, except main dishes, contain no more than 4 grams of fat per serving. Main dish recipes with a ♥ contain no more than 6 grams of fat per serving.

🎖 Prize Winning
These recipes have been winners in The Quaker® Oatmeal Recipe Contest.

👤 Classics
These recipes are old and new favorites of The Quaker® Oatmeal Kitchens. Many have appeared on the Quaker Oats package and are still among our most requested recipes.

Nutrition information for each recipe is provided on pages 92 through 94. This information is based on a nutrition analysis of all ingredients, excluding optional ingredients. When a choice of ingredients is given, the analysis is based on the first ingredient listed.

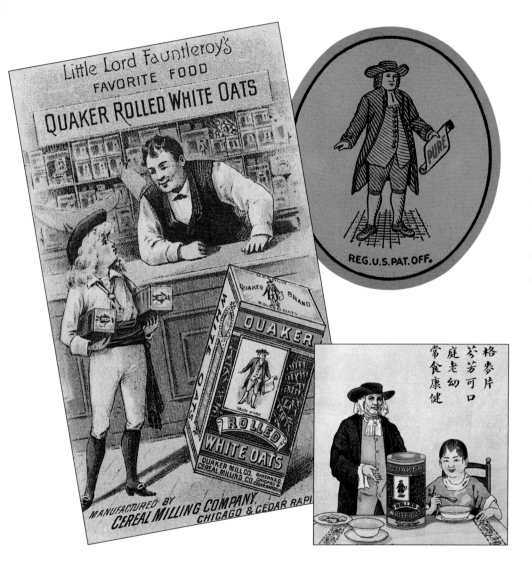

Seventy of our favorite recipes, many with beautiful color photos, have been divided into eight chapters: Cookies, Muffins, Breads, Desserts, Main Dishes, Breakfasts, Celebrations and Kids. Classic Quaker Oats recipes like *Quaker's Best Oatmeal Cookies* and *Prize-Winning Meatloaf* are sprinkled throughout the book as are newer recipes, many of which are lower in fat, cholesterol and sodium than their more traditional counterparts. If you love to bake, you're sure

OATMEAL TRAVELS THE WORLD

Oatmeal has traveled to the North Pole with Admiral Richard Byrd, to the South Pole with Roald Amundsen, and to Mt. Everest with Sir Edmund Hillary. Oatmeal also has orbited the earth with U.S. astronauts. Today, Quaker® Oats remains the largest-selling hot cereal in the United States and is sold in more than 25 countries around the world.

One of the First Convenience Products

In 1921, Quick Quaker® Oats, which cooks in 1 minute, joined Old Fashioned Quaker® Oats on supermarket shelves. Instant Quaker® Oatmeal made its debut in 1966 and is currently available in more than a dozen different flavors. Quaker® Quick 'n Hearty™ Microwave Oatmeal was introduced in 1996. It combines the rich, hearty texture of old fashioned oats with the convenience of instant oatmeal.

Other Firsts

Quaker® Oats also was the first cereal to offer recipes and premiums on its package. In 1919, a radio kit was offered in exchange for $1 and two Quaker Oats trademarks. When assembled, it resembled the Quaker Oats package. This was the earliest radio to enter thousands of American homes.

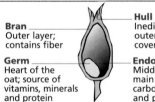

to enjoy savory *Italian Herbed Oatmeal Focaccia*, chocolate-covered *Oatmeal Butter Brittle Cookies* and other winners from The Quaker Oatmeal Recipe Contest.

Because holidays are always a reason to bake something special for those we love, an entire chapter called Celebrations is devoted to recipes for special occasions. There you'll find just the right cookie to celebrate all of life's big and little events. And to provide plenty of afternoons of baking fun, turn to the Kids chapter. *Dinosaur Cookies, Chocolate Cookie Bears, Giant Brownie Ice Cream Sandwich* and other fun-to-make (and eat!) treats will please children of all ages.

From beginning to end, we've filled this book with our favorite recipes, recipes with the whole grain goodness of Quaker Oats that we know you and your family will enjoy again and again.

KNOW YOUR OATS
THE WHOLE (GRAIN) TRUTH

Quaker® Oats (quick, old fashioned and instant) is a whole grain because all three parts of the grain remain after milling: the bran, germ and endosperm.

Bran
Outer layer; contains fiber

Germ
Heart of the oat; source of vitamins, minerals and protein

Hull
Inedible outer covering

Endosperm
Middle layer; main source of carbohydrate and protein

The oat is called a **groat** after the hull has been removed.

Old Fashioned Oats are groats that are steamed and rolled but not cut. They cook in 5 minutes on the stove top or in the microwave oven and can be used for baking.

Quick Oats are groats that are cut into two or three pieces, then steamed and rolled. They cook in just 1 minute and also can be used for baking.

To make **Instant Oatmeal**, the groats are steamed, cut into small pieces, then steamed again and rolled. Available in both regular and a variety of flavors, instant oatmeal can be prepared in the bowl by adding boiling water. It is not recommended for baking.

COOKIES

Peanutty Crisscrosses,
page 20

1¼ cups (2½ sticks) margarine or butter, softened
¾ cup firmly packed brown sugar
½ cup granulated sugar
1 egg
1 teaspoon vanilla
1½ cups all-purpose flour
1 teaspoon baking soda
1 teaspoon ground cinnamon
½ teaspoon salt (optional)
¼ teaspoon ground nutmeg
3 cups Quaker® Oats (quick or old fashioned, uncooked)

TIP· Either margarine or butter can be used to make the recipes in this book. Tub, soft, whipped and reduced-fat or reduced-calorie spreads should *not* be used for baking. The added water and air in these products can cause cookies to be thin, flat and tough.

1 Heat oven to 375°F. Beat margarine and sugars until creamy. Add egg and vanilla; beat well. Add combined flour, baking soda, cinnamon, salt and nutmeg; mix well. Stir in oats; mix well.

2 Drop dough by rounded tablespoonfuls onto ungreased cookie sheets.

3 Bake 8 to 9 minutes for a chewy cookie or 10 to 11 minutes for a crisp cookie. Cool 1 minute on cookie sheets; remove to wire rack. Cool completely. Store tightly covered.

Yield: About 3 dozen

Bar Cookies: Press dough onto bottom of ungreased 13 x 9-inch baking pan. Bake 25 to 30 minutes or until light golden brown. Cool completely; cut into bars. Store tightly covered.
Yield: About 2 dozen

VARIATIONS:
• Stir in 1 cup raisins or chopped nuts.
• Omit spices and stir in 1 cup semisweet chocolate, butterscotch or peanut butter pieces.

CHEWY CHOC-OAT-CHIP™ COOKIES

1 cup (2 sticks) margarine or butter, softened
1 cup firmly packed brown sugar
½ cup granulated sugar
2 eggs
2 tablespoons milk
2 teaspoons vanilla
1¾ cups all-purpose flour
1 teaspoon baking soda
½ teaspoon salt (optional)
2½ cups Quaker® Oats (quick or old fashioned, uncooked)
2 cups (12 ounces) semisweet chocolate pieces
1 cup chopped nuts (optional)

TIP· To measure oats, flour and granulated sugar, lightly spoon into dry nested measuring cup. Using a metal spatula or the straight edge of a table knife, level even with the top of the cup.

1 Heat oven to 375°F. Beat margarine and sugars until creamy. Add eggs, milk and vanilla; beat well. Add combined flour, baking soda and salt; mix well. Stir in oats, chocolate pieces and nuts; mix well.

2 Drop dough by rounded tablespoonfuls onto ungreased cookie sheets.

3 Bake 9 to 10 minutes for a chewy cookie or 12 to 13 minutes for a crisp cookie. Cool 1 minute on cookie sheets; remove to wire rack. Cool completely. Store tightly covered.

Yield: About 5 dozen

Bar Cookies: Press dough onto bottom of ungreased 13 x 9-inch baking pan. Bake 30 to 35 minutes or until light golden brown. Cool completely; cut into bars. Store tightly covered.
Yield: 32 bars

APPLE OATMEAL SPICE COOKIES

¾ **cup firmly packed brown sugar**
½ **cup granulated sugar**
¼ **cup (½ stick) margarine, softened**
¾ **cup apple butter* or applesauce**
2 **egg whites or 1 egg**
2 **tablespoons skim milk**
2 **teaspoons vanilla**
1½ **cups all-purpose flour**
1 **teaspoon baking soda**
1 **teaspoon ground cinnamon**
½ **teaspoon salt (optional)**
¼ **teaspoon ground nutmeg (optional)**
3 **cups Quaker® Oats (quick or old fashioned, uncooked)**
1 **cup diced dried mixed fruit or raisins**

TIP· For a no-fat-added cookie, omit margarine and increase apple butter to 1 cup; continue as recipe directs.

*Look for apple butter in the jam and jelly section of the supermarket.

1 Heat oven to 350°F. Lightly spray cookie sheets with no-stick cooking spray.

2 Beat sugars and margarine until well blended. Add apple butter, egg whites, milk and vanilla; beat well. Add combined flour, baking soda, cinnamon, salt and nutmeg; mix well. Stir in oats and dried fruit; mix well. (Dough will be moist.)

3 Drop dough by rounded tablespoonfuls onto cookie sheets.

4 Bake 10 to 12 minutes or until edges are light golden brown. Cool 1 minute on cookie sheets; remove to wire rack. Cool completely. Store tightly covered.

Yield: About 3½ dozen

FAMOUS OATMEAL COOKIES

1 cup firmly packed brown sugar
¾ cup vegetable shortening (regular or butter flavored)
½ cup granulated sugar
¼ cup water
1 egg
1 teaspoon vanilla
3 cups Quaker® Oats (quick or old fashioned, uncooked)
1 cup all-purpose flour
1 teaspoon salt (optional)
½ teaspoon baking soda

TIP· In most recipes, either Quick or Old Fashioned Quaker® Oats may be used. Old fashioned oats add more texture because the oats are left whole. Instant oatmeal is not recommended for baking.

PERFECT DROP COOKIES

• Use shiny aluminum cookie sheets without rims.

• Preheat oven 10 to 15 minutes before baking.

• After adding flour, don't beat vigorously or overmix dough.

• Use two spoons to scoop and place dough onto the cookie sheets in evenly spaced mounds.

• Leave 2 inches in between so cookies have room to spread.

• Check cookies for doneness after the minimum baking time.

• Cool cookies 1 minute on cookie sheets, then transfer to cooling rack with wide metal spatula.

• Cool cookie sheets completely between batches.

1 Heat oven to 350°F. Beat brown sugar, shortening and granulated sugar until creamy. Add water, egg and vanilla; beat well. Add combined oats, flour, salt and baking soda; mix well.

2 Drop dough by rounded teaspoonfuls onto ungreased cookie sheets.

3 Bake 11 to 13 minutes or until edges are golden brown. Remove to wire rack; cool completely. Store tightly covered.

Yield: About 5 dozen

Bar Cookies: Press dough onto bottom of ungreased 13 x 9-inch baking pan. Bake 30 to 35 minutes or until light golden brown. Cool completely; cut into bars. Store tightly covered. *Yield: About 2 dozen*

Cookies

- 1 cup firmly packed brown sugar
- ¾ cup (1½ sticks) margarine or butter, softened
- 1 cup mashed ripe bananas (about 3 medium)
- 1 egg
- 2 tablespoons grated lemon peel
- 1½ cups all-purpose flour
- 1 teaspoon ground cinnamon
- ½ teaspoon baking soda
- ¼ teaspoon ground ginger
- ¼ teaspoon ground nutmeg
- 1¾ cups Quaker® Oats (quick or old fashioned, uncooked)
- 1½ cups raisins or chopped pitted prunes
- 1 cup chopped walnuts
- ¾ cup chopped pitted dates

Glaze

- 1½ cups powdered sugar
- 3 tablespoons margarine or butter, softened
- 3 tablespoons low-fat milk

1 Heat oven to 375°F. Line cookie sheets with aluminum foil.

2 Beat sugar and margarine until creamy. Add bananas, egg and lemon peel; beat well. Add combined flour, cinnamon, baking soda, ginger and nutmeg; mix well. Stir in oats, raisins, walnuts and dates; mix well.

3 Drop dough by rounded tablespoonfuls onto cookie sheets.

4 Bake 12 to 15 minutes or until light golden brown. (Do not overbake; cookies should remain soft.) Slide cookies and foil from cookie sheets onto wire rack; cool while preparing glaze.

5 Combine glaze ingredients; mix until smooth. (Glaze should be thick.) Spoon small amount of glaze over warm cookies, letting glaze run down sides. Cool completely. Remove cookies from foil. Store tightly covered.

Yield: About 4 dozen

MAKE-AHEAD TIPS FOR DROP COOKIES

- **To Refrigerate Cookie Dough:** Tightly wrap dough in plastic wrap. Refrigerate up to 3 days. Bake according to directions.*

- **To Freeze Cookie Dough:** Pack dough into airtight container or resealable freezer bag, removing as much air as possible. Seal, label and freeze up to 4 months. Thaw in refrigerator (about 8 hours). Bake according to directions.*

- **To Freeze Baked Cookies:** Cool cookies completely. Place cookies in airtight containers or resealable freezer bags. Seal, label and freeze up to 4 months. Thaw cookies, covered, at room temperature.

*Baking times may be longer because dough is cold.

OATMEAL MACAROONS

COOKIE SHEETS & BAKING PANS

- For best results, use shiny aluminum cookie sheets without rims and shiny metal baking pans.

- Cookies baked on insulated cookie sheets require more baking time and take longer to brown. Cookies baked on dark-surfaced cookie sheets require a shorter baking time and brown more quickly.

- To substitute a glass baking dish for a metal baking pan of the same size, reduce oven temperature by 25°F.

  1 cup (2 sticks) margarine or butter, softened
  1 cup firmly packed brown sugar
  2 eggs
 ½ teaspoon almond extract
1¼ cups all-purpose flour
  1 teaspoon baking soda
  3 cups Quaker® Oats (quick or old fashioned, uncooked)
1⅓ cups shredded coconut

1 Heat oven to 350°F. Lightly grease cookie sheets.

2 Beat margarine and sugar until creamy. Add eggs and almond extract; beat well. Add combined flour and baking soda; mix well. Stir in oats and coconut; mix well.

3 Drop dough by rounded teaspoonfuls onto cookie sheets.

4 Bake 8 minutes or until light golden brown. Cool 2 minutes on cookie sheets; remove to wire rack. Cool completely. Store tightly covered.

Yield: About 4 dozen

1 cup (2 sticks) margarine or butter, softened
¾ cup granulated sugar
¾ cup firmly packed brown sugar
2 eggs
1 teaspoon vanilla
1¼ cups all-purpose flour
1 teaspoon baking soda
½ teaspoon salt (optional)
3 cups Quaker® Oats (quick or old fashioned, uncooked)
2 cups (12 ounces) butterscotch pieces

1 Heat oven to 375°F. Beat margarine, sugars, eggs and vanilla until creamy. Add combined flour, baking soda and salt; mix well. Stir in oats and butterscotch pieces; mix well.

2 Drop dough by level tablespoonfuls onto ungreased cookie sheets.

3 Bake 7 to 8 minutes for a chewy cookie or 9 to 10 minutes for a crisp cookie. Cool 2 minutes on cookie sheets; remove to wire rack. Cool completely. Store tightly covered.

Yield: 4 dozen

TIP· For easier mixing, let margarine or butter stand at room temperature until it's soft enough to blend smoothly with other ingredients. To speed up softening, cut cold margarine or butter into small pieces and beat with an electric mixer. To soften in the microwave oven, microwave 1 stick (unwrapped) at a time on the lowest power setting, checking every 10 to 15 seconds.

COCOA OATMEAL COOKIES

1 cup (2 sticks) margarine or butter, softened
1 cup firmly packed brown sugar
½ cup granulated sugar
2 eggs
1 teaspoon vanilla
1½ cups all-purpose flour
⅓ cup unsweetened cocoa powder
1 teaspoon baking soda
½ teaspoon salt (optional)
3 cups Quaker® Oats (quick or old fashioned, uncooked)
1 cup raisins (optional)

1 Heat oven to 350°F. Beat margarine and sugars until creamy. Add eggs and vanilla; beat well. Add combined flour, cocoa powder, baking soda and salt; mix well. Stir in oats and raisins; mix well.

2 Drop dough by rounded tablespoonfuls onto ungreased cookie sheets.

3 Bake 10 to 12 minutes or until cookies are almost set. (Do not overbake.) Cool 1 minute on cookie sheets; remove to wire rack. Cool completely. Store tightly covered.

Yield: About 4 dozen

2 cups Quaker® Oats (quick or old fashioned, uncooked)

1¼ cups all-purpose flour

½ teaspoon baking powder

1 cup (2 sticks) butter or margarine, chilled and cut into pieces

1 cup powdered sugar

⅔ cup firmly packed brown sugar

1½ tablespoons water

1 teaspoon vanilla

1 cup chopped dry roasted or lightly salted peanuts

2 cups (12 ounces) semisweet chocolate pieces

1 Heat oven to 350°F. Line two cookie sheets with aluminum foil.

2 Combine oats, flour and baking powder. Add butter; beat on low to medium speed of electric mixer until crumbly. Add powdered sugar, brown sugar, water and vanilla. Beat on low speed until dough starts to form. By hand, stir in peanuts.

3 Divide dough in half. Place half on one cookie sheet; flatten with lightly floured hands into 13 x 9-inch rectangle. Repeat using remaining dough and second cookie sheet.

4 Bake 22 to 25 minutes or until golden brown, rotating cookie sheets after 12 minutes. Remove cookie sheets to wire racks.

5 Sprinkle 1 cup chocolate pieces evenly over each large cookie. Let stand 2 to 3 minutes. With spatula or knife, spread softened chocolate evenly over cookies. Cool completely. (Chill 15 minutes to set chocolate, if necessary.)

6 Remove large cookies from cookie sheets and peel off foil. Break each into 24 pieces. Store tightly covered.

Yield: About 4 dozen

TECHNIQUE: To rotate cookie sheets:
1. Move the cookie sheet on the top oven rack to the bottom rack and vice versa.
2. Turn both cookie sheets so the fronts of the sheets are facing the back of the oven.

1995 Grand Prize—Gloria Piantek, Plainsboro, NJ

LEMON WAFERS

1¼ cups granulated sugar

½ cup (1 stick) margarine, softened

½ cup plain nonfat yogurt or lemon low-fat yogurt

2 egg whites or 1 egg

1 tablespoon grated lemon peel

½ teaspoon vanilla

2 cups Quaker® Oats (quick or old fashioned, uncooked)

1½ cups all-purpose flour

1 teaspoon baking powder

½ teaspoon baking soda

Granulated sugar

¼ cup powdered sugar

1 Beat 1¼ cups granulated sugar and margarine until creamy. Add yogurt, egg whites, lemon peel and vanilla; beat well. Gradually add combined oats, flour, baking powder and baking soda; mix well. Cover; chill 1 to 3 hours.

2 Heat oven to 375°F. Lightly spray cookie sheets with no-stick cooking spray.

3 With lightly floured hands, shape dough into 1-inch balls. Place 3 inches apart on cookie sheets. Flatten to ⅛ inch thickness with bottom of glass dipped in granulated sugar.

4 Bake 10 to 12 minutes or until edges are lightly browned. Cool 2 minutes on cookie sheets; remove to wire rack.

5 Sift powdered sugar over warm cookies. Cool completely. Store tightly covered.

Yield: About 4 dozen

1¼ cups firmly packed brown sugar
 1 cup (2 sticks) margarine or butter, softened
 2 eggs
 2 tablespoons molasses
 1 teaspoon maple extract
1¼ cups all-purpose flour
 1 teaspoon baking soda
2½ cups Quaker® Oats (quick or old fashioned, uncooked)
 1 cup pecans, coarsely chopped
 ¾ cup pecan halves (about 48 halves)

TIP · Either light or dark molasses may be used in this recipe. Light molasses has a milder flavor and lighter color.

1 Beat sugar and margarine until creamy. Add eggs, molasses and maple extract; beat well. Add combined flour and baking soda; mix well. Stir in oats and chopped pecans; mix well. Cover; chill at least 1 hour.

2 Heat oven to 350°F. Lightly grease cookie sheets.

3 Shape dough into 1-inch balls. Place 3 inches apart on cookie sheets. Flatten each ball by pressing a pecan half in the center.

4 Bake 10 to 12 minutes or until deep golden brown. Immediately remove to wire rack; cool completely. Store tightly covered.

Yield: About 4 dozen

1993 First Prize—Cookies
Betty Freeman, Sherman Oaks, CA

PEANUTTY CRISSCROSSES

1½ **cups firmly packed brown sugar**
1 **cup peanut butter**
¾ **cup (1½ sticks) margarine or butter, softened**
⅓ **cup water**
1 **egg**
1 **teaspoon vanilla**
3 **cups Quaker® Oats (quick or old fashioned, uncooked)**
1½ **cups all-purpose flour**
½ **teaspoon baking soda**
  Granulated sugar

TIP· For best results, use regular peanut butter, either creamy or crunchy-style. Reduced-fat peanut butter is not recommended for baking.

1 Beat sugar, peanut butter and margarine until creamy. Add water, egg and vanilla; beat well. Add combined oats, flour and baking soda; mix well. Cover; chill about 2 hours.

2 Heat oven to 350°F. Shape dough into 1-inch balls. Place 2 inches apart on ungreased cookie sheets. Flatten with tines of fork dipped in granulated sugar to form criss-cross pattern.

3 Bake 9 to 10 minutes or until edges are golden brown. Cool 2 minutes on cookie sheets; remove to wire rack. Cool completely. Store tightly covered.

Yield: About 7 dozen

BLUEBERRY STREUSEL BARS

1½ cups Quaker® Oats (quick or old fashioned, uncooked)
1¼ cups all-purpose flour
½ cup firmly packed brown sugar
¾ cup (1½ sticks) margarine or butter, melted
1 cup fresh or frozen blueberries (do not thaw)
⅓ cup raspberry or strawberry preserves
1 teaspoon all-purpose flour
½ teaspoon grated lemon peel (optional)

1 Heat oven to 350°F. Combine oats, flour, sugar and margarine; mix until crumbly. Reserve 1 cup oat mixture for topping; set aside. Press remaining oat mixture onto bottom of ungreased 8 or 9-inch square baking pan. Bake 13 to 15 minutes or until light golden brown. Cool slightly.

2 In medium bowl, combine blueberries, preserves, flour and lemon peel; mix gently. Spread over crust. Sprinkle with reserved oat mixture, patting gently.

3 Bake 20 to 22 minutes or until light golden brown. Cool completely. Cut into bars. Store tightly covered.

Yield: 16 bars

CARAMEL OATMEAL CHEWIES

PERFECT BAR COOKIES

....

- Use a shiny metal baking pan in the exact size specified in the recipe.

- Use your fingers or the back of a large spoon to press stiff doughs into pan; use a spatula to spread batters evenly into pan. Use fingers to pat oatmeal and crumb crusts onto bottom of pan.

- When testing bar cookies for doneness, your best guides are time and appearance. Use a timer and check after the minimum baking time.

- Cool bar cookies in their pan on a wire cooling rack.

1¾ cups Quaker® Oats (quick or old fashioned, uncooked)
1½ cups all-purpose flour
¾ cup firmly packed brown sugar
½ teaspoon baking soda
¼ teaspoon salt (optional)
¾ cup (1½ sticks) margarine or butter, melted
1 cup chopped nuts
1 cup (6 ounces) semisweet chocolate pieces
1 cup butterscotch caramel fudge topping
¼ cup all-purpose flour

1 Heat oven to 350°F. Lightly grease 13 x 9-inch baking pan.

2 In large bowl, combine oats, 1½ cups flour, sugar, baking soda and salt; mix well. Stir in margarine; mix well. Reserve 1 cup oat mixture for topping; set aside. Press remaining oat mixture onto bottom of pan. Bake 10 to 12 minutes or until light golden brown; cool 10 minutes.

3 Sprinkle nuts and chocolate pieces evenly over partially baked crust. Combine butterscotch caramel topping and ¼ cup flour; mix until smooth. Drizzle over chocolate pieces to within ¼ inch of edges. Sprinkle with reserved oat mixture, patting gently.

4 Bake 18 to 22 minutes or until golden brown. Cool; chill until firm. Cut into bars. Store tightly covered.

Yield: 32 bars

1¼ cups all-purpose flour
1¼ cups Quaker® Oats (quick or old fashioned, uncooked)
⅓ cup granulated sugar
⅓ cup firmly packed brown sugar
½ teaspoon baking powder
¼ teaspoon salt (optional)
¾ cup (1½ sticks) margarine or butter, chilled and cut into pieces
¼ cup chopped almonds (optional)
¾ cup raspberry preserves
1 cup (6 ounces) semisweet chocolate pieces

½ cup (3 ounces) vanilla milk chips or semisweet chocolate pieces (optional)

1 Heat oven to 375°F. In large bowl, combine flour, oats, sugars, baking powder and salt. Cut in margarine* with pastry blender or two knives until mixture is crumbly. Reserve 1 cup oat mixture for topping; stir in almonds. Set aside. Press remaining oat mixture onto bottom of ungreased 8-inch square baking pan. Bake 10 minutes.

2 Spread preserves evenly over partially baked crust to within ¼ inch of edges; sprinkle evenly with 1 cup chocolate pieces. Sprinkle reserved oat mixture over chocolate pieces, patting gently. Bake 30 to 35 minutes or until golden brown. Cool completely.

3 If desired, melt vanilla milk chips according to package directions. Drizzle over top. Let stand until set. Cut into squares. Store tightly covered.

Yield: 36 squares

*For an explanation of this technique, see page 37.

1992 Honorable Mention—Cookies
Daniella Nixon, Enfield, CT

OATMEAL DREAM DATES

One 8-ounce package pitted dates, coarsely chopped
1½ cups orange juice
2½ cups all-purpose flour
1½ cups firmly packed brown sugar
½ teaspoon salt (optional)
1½ cups (3 sticks) margarine or butter, chilled and cut into pieces
2 cups Quaker® Oats (quick or old fashioned, uncooked)
1½ cups shredded coconut, divided
1 cup chopped walnuts or pecans

1 In medium saucepan, combine dates and orange juice. Bring to a boil; reduce heat. Simmer 15 to 20 minutes or until thickened, stirring occasionally. Remove from heat; cool slightly.

2 Heat oven to 350°F. In large bowl, combine flour, sugar and salt. Cut in margarine* with pastry blender or two knives until mixture is crumbly. Stir in oats, 1 cup coconut and walnuts; mix well. Reserve 4 cups oat mixture for topping; set aside. Press remaining oat mixture onto bottom of ungreased 13 x 9-inch baking pan.

3 Spread date mixture evenly over crust to within ¼ inch of edges. Sprinkle with reserved oat mixture. Sprinkle with remaining ½ cup coconut, patting gently.

4 Bake 35 to 40 minutes or until light golden brown. Cool completely. Cut into bars. Store tightly covered.

Yield: 36 bars

*For an explanation of this technique, see page 37.

1994 First Prize—Cookies
Anne Altaner, Ft. Lauderdale, FL

MUFFINS

*Quaker's Best
Oatmeal Muffins
and variations,
page 31*

LEMON BLUEBERRY OATMEAL MUFFINS

Topping
- ¼ cup Quaker® Oats (quick or old fashioned, uncooked)
- 2 tablespoons sugar

Muffins
- 1½ cups Quaker® Oats (quick or old fashioned, uncooked)
- 1 cup all-purpose flour
- ½ cup sugar
- 1 tablespoon baking powder
- ¼ teaspoon salt (optional)
- 1 cup skim milk
- 2 egg whites or 1 egg, lightly beaten
- 2 tablespoons vegetable oil
- 1 teaspoon grated lemon peel
- 1 teaspoon vanilla
- 1 cup fresh or frozen blueberries (do not thaw)

1 Heat oven to 400°F. Line 12 medium muffin cups with paper baking cups or spray bottoms only with no-stick cooking spray.

2 Combine topping ingredients; mix well. Set aside.

3 In large bowl, combine oats, flour, sugar, baking powder and salt; mix well. In small bowl, combine milk, egg whites, oil, lemon peel and vanilla; blend well. Add to dry ingredients all at once; stir just until dry ingredients are moistened. (Do not overmix.) Gently fold in* blueberries.

4 Fill muffin cups almost full. Sprinkle with reserved topping, patting gently.

5 Bake 20 to 24 minutes or until light golden brown. Cool muffins in pan on wire rack 5 minutes; remove from pan. Serve warm.

Yield: 1 dozen

*For an explanation of this technique, see page 53.

Topping

- ¼ cup Quaker® Oats (quick or old fashioned, uncooked)
- 1 tablespoon firmly packed brown sugar
- 1 tablespoon margarine, melted
- ⅛ teaspoon ground cinnamon

Muffins

- 1½ cups Quaker® Oats (quick or old fashioned, uncooked)
- 1¼ cups all-purpose flour
- 1 teaspoon baking powder
- ¾ teaspoon baking soda
- ¾ teaspoon ground cinnamon
- 1 cup unsweetened applesauce
- ½ cup skim milk
- ½ cup firmly packed brown sugar
- 3 tablespoons vegetable oil
- 1 egg white, lightly beaten

1 Heat oven to 400°F. Line 12 medium muffin cups with paper baking cups or spray bottoms only with no-stick cooking spray.

2 Combine topping ingredients; mix well. Set aside.

3 In large bowl, combine oats, flour, baking powder, baking soda and cinnamon; mix well. In small bowl, combine applesauce, milk, sugar, oil and egg white; blend well. Add to dry ingredients all at once; stir just until dry ingredients are moistened. (Do not overmix.)

4 Fill muffin cups almost full. Sprinkle with reserved topping, patting gently.

5 Bake 20 to 22 minutes or until deep golden brown. Cool muffins in pan on wire rack 5 minutes; remove from pan. Serve warm.

Yield: 1 dozen

PERFECT MUFFINS

- Grease muffin cups as directed in recipe, or line with paper baking cups.

- Thoroughly combine dry ingredients in one bowl and liquid ingredients in a second bowl.

- Add liquid ingredients to dry ingredients all at once and stir *just* until dry ingredients are moistened. There should be some lumps.

- Immediately spoon batter into muffin cups and bake in a preheated oven.

- Test for doneness by inserting a wooden pick into the center of a muffin. If pick comes out with a few moist crumbs clinging to it, the muffins are done. If batter clings to pick, bake 2 minutes and test again.

- Cool muffins in pan on rack 5 minutes; remove and serve warm.

WHOLE GRAIN BANANA MUFFINS

1½ cups all-purpose flour

1 cup Quaker® Oats (quick or old fashioned, uncooked)

½ cup firmly packed brown sugar

½ cup chopped walnuts (optional)

1 tablespoon baking powder

½ teaspoon baking soda

1 cup mashed ripe bananas (about 3 medium)

½ cup skim milk

⅓ cup (5 tablespoons plus 1 teaspoon) margarine or butter, melted

2 egg whites or 1 egg, lightly beaten

TIP • Really ripe bananas give baked products the most intense flavor. Look for bananas that are deep yellow and speckled with brown. Three medium bananas (about 1 pound) equal 1 cup mashed bananas.

1 Heat oven to 400°F. Line 12 medium muffin cups with paper baking cups or spray bottoms only with no-stick cooking spray.

2 In large bowl, combine flour, oats, sugar, walnuts, baking powder and baking soda; mix well. In small bowl, combine bananas, milk, margarine and egg whites; blend well. Add to dry ingredients all at once; stir just until dry ingredients are moistened. (Do not overmix.)

3 Fill muffin cups almost full. Bake 17 to 19 minutes or until golden brown. Cool muffins in pan on wire rack 5 minutes; remove from pan. Serve warm.

Yield: 1 dozen

FREEZING MUFFINS

All of the muffins in this book may be frozen.

- To freeze, wrap cooled muffins securely in foil, or place in freezer bag. Seal, label and freeze up to 6 months.

- To reheat in microwave oven, place unwrapped muffin on napkin, microwave-safe paper towel or plate. Microwave on HIGH about 30 seconds for each muffin.

- To reheat in conventional oven, heat foil-wrapped muffins at 350°F 15 to 20 minutes.

Honey Lime Oat Muffins

Muffins
- 1 cup Quaker® Oats (quick or old fashioned, uncooked)
- One 8-ounce container plain nonfat or low-fat yogurt
- ½ cup honey
- ¼ cup skim milk
- 3 tablespoons margarine, melted
- 2 teaspoons grated lime peel
- 2 egg whites, lightly beaten
- 1½ cups all-purpose flour
- ½ teaspoon baking soda
- ¼ teaspoon salt (optional)

Glaze
- ¾ cup powdered sugar
- 4 teaspoons fresh lime juice
- 1 teaspoon grated lime peel

1 Heat oven to 375°F. Line 12 medium muffin cups with paper baking cups or spray bottoms only with no-stick cooking spray.

2 In large bowl, combine oats, yogurt, honey, milk, margarine and lime peel; mix well. Let stand 10 minutes. Stir in egg whites until blended.

3 In medium bowl, combine flour, baking soda and salt; mix well. Add to oat mixture all at once; stir just until dry ingredients are moistened. (Do not overmix.)

4 Fill muffin cups almost full. Bake 20 to 24 minutes or until light golden brown. Cool muffins in pan on wire rack 5 minutes; remove from pan. Cool 10 minutes.

5 Combine glaze ingredients; mix until smooth. Dip tops of muffins into glaze. Serve warm.

Yield: 1 dozen

29

PLUM ALMOND MUFFINS

Topping

- 3 tablespoons Quaker® Oats (quick or old fashioned, uncooked)
- 2 tablespoons sliced almonds (optional)
- 1 tablespoon sugar
- 1 tablespoon margarine, melted

Muffins

- 1½ cups Quaker® Oats (quick or old fashioned, uncooked)
- 1¼ cups all-purpose flour
- ½ cup sugar
- 2 teaspoons baking powder
- ½ teaspoon ground cinnamon
- ¼ teaspoon salt (optional)
- 1 cup skim milk
- 3 tablespoons margarine or butter, melted
- 2 egg whites or 1 egg, lightly beaten
- ¼ to ½ teaspoon almond extract
- ¾ cup unpeeled, finely chopped fresh plums (about 3 medium)

VARIATION: Substitute peaches or nectarines for plums.

1 Heat oven to 400°F. Line 12 medium muffin cups with paper baking cups or spray bottoms only with no-stick cooking spray.

2 Combine topping ingredients; mix well. Set aside.

3 In large bowl, combine oats, flour, sugar, baking powder, cinnamon and salt; mix well. In small bowl, combine milk, margarine, egg whites and almond extract; blend well. Add to dry ingredients all at once; stir just until dry ingredients are moistened. (Do not overmix.) Gently fold in* plums.

4 Fill muffin cups almost full. Sprinkle with reserved topping, patting gently.

5 Bake 20 to 22 minutes or until light golden brown. Cool muffins in pan on wire rack 5 minutes; remove from pan. Serve warm.

Yield: 1 dozen

*For an explanation of this technique, see page 53.

Topping

- ⅓ cup Quaker® Oats (quick or old fashioned, uncooked)
- ¼ cup all-purpose flour
- ¼ cup firmly packed brown sugar
- 3 tablespoons margarine or butter, chilled

Muffins

- 1½ cups all-purpose flour
- 1 cup Quaker® Oats (quick or old fashioned, uncooked)
- ½ cup granulated sugar
- 1 tablespoon baking powder
- 1 cup low-fat milk
- ¼ cup vegetable oil
- 1 egg, lightly beaten
- 1 teaspoon vanilla

1 Heat oven to 400°F. Line 12 medium muffin cups with paper baking cups.

2 Combine oats, flour and sugar for topping; mix well. Cut in margarine* with pastry blender or two knives until mixture is crumbly; set aside.

3 In large bowl, combine flour, oats, sugar and baking powder; mix well. In small bowl, combine milk, oil, egg and vanilla; blend well. Add to dry ingredients all at once; stir just until dry ingredients are moistened. (Do not overmix.)

4 Fill muffin cups three-fourths full. Sprinkle with reserved topping, patting gently.

5 Bake 18 to 20 minutes or until golden brown. Cool muffins in pan on wire rack 5 minutes; remove from pan. Serve warm.

Yield: 1 dozen

*For an explanation of this technique, see page 37.

VARIATIONS:

- *Chocolate Surprise Muffins:* Increase sugar to ⅔ cup and add ¼ cup unsweetened cocoa powder to dry ingredients. Fill muffin cups half full. Spoon 1 teaspoon cherry preserves in center of each; top with remaining batter. Omit topping. Sprinkle muffins with powdered sugar.

- *Cranberry Muffins:* Add 1 cup chopped cranberries to dry ingredients. Omit topping. Drizzle *Citrus Glaze* over muffins: Combine ¾ cup powdered sugar, 4 teaspoons orange juice and 1 teaspoon grated orange peel.

- *Star Spangled Muffins:* Stir ½ cup *each* blueberries and sliced strawberries into batter. Omit topping; sprinkle batter-filled cups with cinnamon-sugar.

BREADS

*Quaker's Best
Oatmeal Bread,*
page 39

2 cups all-purpose flour
1 cup Quaker® Oats (quick or old fashioned, uncooked)
¾ cup sugar
1 teaspoon baking powder
½ teaspoon baking soda
½ teaspoon salt (optional)
¾ cup chopped fresh, frozen (thawed) or dried cranberries
½ cup chopped walnuts or pecans (optional)
¾ cup low-fat milk
⅓ cup orange juice
⅓ cup vegetable oil
3 eggs, lightly beaten
1 tablespoon grated orange peel

TIP · To bring out their flavor, lightly toast nuts. To toast, spread nuts evenly in shallow baking pan. Bake at 350°F for 5 to 10 minutes or until light golden brown, stirring occasionally. Cool completely before using.

1 Heat oven to 350°F. Grease and flour bottom only of 9 x 5-inch loaf pan.

2 In large bowl, combine flour, oats, sugar, baking powder, baking soda and salt; mix well. Stir in cranberries and walnuts. In medium bowl, combine milk, orange juice, oil, eggs and orange peel; blend well. Add to dry ingredients all at once; stir just until dry ingredients are moistened. (Do not overmix.) Pour into pan.

3 Bake 60 to 70 minutes or until wooden pick inserted in center comes out clean. Cool 10 minutes in pan; remove to wire rack. Cool completely.

Yield: 1 loaf (12 servings)

PERFECT QUICK BREAD LOAVES

- **Grease pan as directed in recipe. When pan sides are not greased, quick bread batters can climb higher and form a more rounded top.**

- **Measure accurately and check the expiration dates on packages of baking powder and baking soda to be sure they are fresh.**

- **Mix the dry ingredients with the liquid ingredients only until the dry ingredients are moistened. Overmixing can make quick breads tough.**

- **Cool bread in pan on wire cooling rack 10 minutes. Loosen sides with metal spatula and turn out onto cooling rack. Cool completely.**

- **Don't worry if the baked loaf has a crack. A lengthwise crack is characteristic of many loaf-type quick breads.**

OATMEAL CARROT CAKE BREAD

Bread

1	cup Quaker® Oats (quick or old fashioned, uncooked)
½	cup skim milk
2½	cups all-purpose flour
1	cup firmly packed brown sugar
1	tablespoon baking powder
½	teaspoon baking soda
½	teaspoon ground cinnamon
¼	teaspoon salt (optional)
1½	cups shredded carrots (about 3 medium)
½	cup raisins
One	8-ounce can crushed pineapple in juice, undrained
4	egg whites or 2 eggs, lightly beaten
¼	cup vegetable oil
1	teaspoon vanilla

Cream Cheese Spread (optional)

4	ounces light cream cheese, softened
2	teaspoons firmly packed brown sugar
¼	teaspoon vanilla

TIP · To soften cream cheese, place in microwaveable bowl. Microwave on HIGH 15 to 30 seconds or until softened.

1 Heat oven to 350°F. Lightly spray bottom only of 9 x 5-inch loaf pan with no-stick cooking spray. In medium bowl, combine oats and milk; mix well. Set aside.

2 In large bowl, combine flour, sugar, baking powder, baking soda, cinnamon and salt; mix well. Stir in carrots and raisins.

3 Add pineapple (including juice), egg whites, oil and vanilla to oat mixture; mix well. Add to dry ingredients all at once; stir just until dry ingredients are moistened. (Do not overmix.) Pour into pan.

4 Bake 60 to 75 minutes or until wooden pick inserted in center comes out clean. Cool 10 minutes in pan; remove to wire rack. Cool completely.

5 Combine ingredients for cream cheese spread; mix until smooth. Serve with bread. Store tightly covered in refrigerator up to 3 days.

Yield: 1 loaf (16 servings)

LOWER-FAT BAKING

We've trimmed the fat in all of the recipes marked with a ♥. You can skinny up your own family favorites by following the tips below. Because reducing the fat in baked products can affect both texture and flavor, be sure to make just one change at a time and keep the changes small.

- **Replace whole eggs with egg whites or egg substitute (1 egg = 2 egg whites or ¼ cup egg substitute).**

- **Substitute skim or 1% low-fat milk for whole milk, light sour cream for sour cream and light cream cheese for cream cheese.**

- **Replace half of the margarine or oil with applesauce, mashed bananas or another fruit purée.**

- **In muffin recipes, reduce the amount of oil 1 tablespoon at a time. Some recipes will be acceptable with only 2 tablespoons oil.**

FESTIVE EGGNOG BREAD

SERVING/ STORAGE TIPS

- Cool bread completely before slicing.

- Cut bread with a sharp, thin-bladed or serrated knife. Use a gentle sawing motion to prevent crumbling.

- If bread will be eaten in a day or two, wrap in foil or plastic wrap. For longer storage, wrap loaf securely in foil, or place in freezer bag. Seal, label and freeze up to 6 months. Thaw at room temperature before serving.

Bread

2	cups all-purpose flour
1	cup Quaker® Oats (quick or old fashioned, uncooked)
¾	cup granulated sugar
1	teaspoon baking powder
½	teaspoon baking soda
¼	teaspoon salt (optional)
¾	cup raisins
1	cup eggnog
2	eggs, lightly beaten
⅓	cup vegetable oil
2	teaspoons rum extract

Glaze

¾	cup powdered sugar
¼ to ½	teaspoon rum extract
1 to 2	tablespoons eggnog

1 Heat oven to 350°F. Grease and flour bottom only of 9 x 5-inch loaf pan.

2 In large bowl, combine flour, oats, sugar, baking powder, baking soda and salt; mix well. Stir in raisins. In medium bowl, combine eggnog, eggs, oil and rum extract; blend well. Add to dry ingredients all at once; stir just until dry ingredients are moistened. (Do not overmix.) Pour into pan.

3 Bake 60 to 70 minutes or until wooden pick inserted in center comes out clean. Cool 10 minutes in pan; remove to wire rack. Cool completely.

4 Combine powdered sugar, rum extract and enough eggnog for desired consistency; mix until smooth. Drizzle over top of loaf.

Yield: 1 loaf (12 servings)

PEAR GINGER SCONES

 BREADS

1 cup all-purpose flour
1 cup Quaker® Oats (quick or old fashioned, uncooked)
⅓ cup plus 2 teaspoons sugar, divided
1½ teaspoons baking powder
1 teaspoon ground ginger
½ teaspoon baking soda
¼ teaspoon ground cinnamon
¼ teaspoon ground nutmeg
¼ teaspoon salt (optional)
3 tablespoons margarine, chilled and cut into pieces
⅔ cup plain nonfat yogurt
2 egg whites or 1 egg, lightly beaten
1 teaspoon vanilla
½ cup unpeeled, finely chopped fresh pear (about 1 medium)

TIP · Bartlett, Anjou and Bosc pears are recommended for baking.

1 Heat oven to 400°F. Lightly spray cookie sheet with no-stick cooking spray.

2 In large bowl, combine flour, oats, ⅓ cup sugar, baking powder, ginger, baking soda, cinnamon, nutmeg and salt; mix well. Cut in margarine with pastry blender or two knives until mixture resembles coarse crumbs. In small bowl, combine yogurt, egg whites and vanilla; blend well. Add to dry ingredients all at once; stir with fork just until dry ingredients are moistened. Gently stir in chopped pear.

3 Drop dough by ¼ cupfuls 2 inches apart on cookie sheet. Sprinkle with remaining 2 teaspoons sugar.

4 Bake 16 to 18 minutes or until light golden brown. Serve warm.

Yield: 10 scones

TECHNIQUE: CUTTING IN

When making scones and biscuits as well as some cookies and cakes, the fat is distributed throughout the dry ingredients using a technique called "cutting in." Using a pastry blender, two knives in a scissors motion or your fingertips, work chilled margarine, butter or shortening into the combined dry ingredients until mixture resembles coarse crumbs.

SCOTTISH OAT SCONES

1½ cups all-purpose flour

1 cup Quaker® Oats (quick or old fashioned, uncooked)

¼ cup sugar

1 tablespoon baking powder

¼ teaspoon salt (optional)

½ cup (1 stick) margarine or butter, chilled and cut into pieces

½ cup currants, raisins, diced dried mixed fruit, dried cranberries or dried blueberries

⅓ cup low-fat milk

1 egg, lightly beaten

1 tablespoon sugar

⅛ teaspoon ground cinnamon

TIP · Leftover scones may be frozen. Cool completely, then wrap securely in foil or place in freezer bag. Seal, label and freeze up to 3 months. To reheat, unwrap and microwave on HIGH about 30 seconds per scone.

1 Heat oven to 400°F. Lightly grease cookie sheet.

2 In large bowl, combine flour, oats, ¼ cup sugar, baking powder and salt; mix well. Cut in margarine with pastry blender or two knives until mixture resembles coarse crumbs. Stir in currants. In small bowl, combine milk and egg; blend well. Add to dry ingredients all at once; stir with fork just until dry ingredients are moistened.

3 Turn dough out onto lightly floured surface; knead gently 8 to 10 times. Roll or pat dough into 8-inch circle about ½ inch thick. Sprinkle with combined 1 tablespoon sugar and cinnamon. Cut into 10 wedges; place on cookie sheet.

4 Bake 12 to 15 minutes or until light golden brown. Serve warm.

Yield: 10 scones

5¾ to 6¼ **cups all-purpose flour**

2½ **cups Quaker® Oats (quick or old fashioned, uncooked)**

¼ **cup sugar**

Two **¼-ounce packages (about 4½ teaspoons) quick-rising yeast**

2½ **teaspoons salt**

1½ **cups water**

1¼ **cups low-fat milk**

¼ **cup (½ stick) margarine**

1 In large bowl, combine 3 cups flour, oats, sugar, yeast and salt; mix well.

2 Heat water, milk and margarine until very warm (120°F to 130°F). Add to flour mixture and blend on low speed of electric mixer until moistened. Beat 3 minutes at medium speed. Stir in enough of the remaining flour to make a stiff dough.

3 Turn dough out onto lightly floured surface. Knead 5 to 8 minutes or until smooth and elastic. Shape dough into ball; place in greased bowl, turning once. Cover; let rise in warm place 30 minutes or until doubled in size.

4 Punch dough down. Cover; let rest 10 minutes. Divide dough in half; shape to form two loaves. Place in two greased 8 x 4 or 9 x 5-inch loaf pans. Brush dough lightly with additional melted margarine; sprinkle with additional oats, if desired. Cover; let rise in warm place 10 to 15 minutes or until nearly doubled in size.

5 Heat oven to 375°F. Bake 45 to 50 minutes or until dark golden brown. Remove from pans to wire rack. Cool completely.

Yield: 2 loaves

ITALIAN HERBED OATMEAL FOCACCIA

1995 First Prize—Breads
Edwina Gadsby, Great Falls, MT

2	tablespoons corn meal
1½ to 2¼	cups all-purpose flour
1	cup Quaker® Oats (quick or old fashioned, uncooked)
2	tablespoons Italian seasoning, divided
One	¼-ounce package (about 2¼ teaspoons) quick-rising yeast
2	teaspoons sugar
1½	teaspoons garlic salt, divided
1	cup water
¼	cup plus 2 tablespoons olive oil, divided
4 to 6	sun-dried tomatoes packed in oil, drained and chopped
¼	cup shredded Parmesan cheese

1 Lightly spray 13 x 9-inch baking pan with no-stick cooking spray; sprinkle with corn meal.

2 In large bowl, combine 1 cup flour, oats, 1 tablespoon Italian seasoning, yeast, sugar and 1 teaspoon garlic salt; mix well.

3 Heat water and ¼ cup oil until very warm (120°F to 130°F). Add to flour mixture; mix well. Gradually stir in enough of the remaining flour to make a soft dough.

4 Turn dough out onto lightly floured surface. Knead 8 to 10 minutes or until smooth and elastic. Cover; let rest 10 minutes.

5 Pat dough into pan, pressing dough out to edges of pan. Using fingertips, poke indentations over surface of dough. Brush remaining 2 tablespoons oil over dough. Sprinkle with remaining 1 tablespoon Italian seasoning and ½ teaspoon garlic salt. Arrange tomatoes across top; sprinkle with cheese.

6 Cover; let rise in warm place until doubled in size, about 30 minutes.

7 Heat oven to 400°F. Bake 25 to 30 minutes or until golden brown. Cut into strips or squares. Serve warm.

Yield: 12 servings

PERFECT YEAST BREADS

- Be sure the yeast is fresh by checking the expiration date on the package.

- Test the temperature of the liquid ingredients with an instant-read thermometer. If the yeast is dissolved in the liquid, the temperature should be warm (105°F to 115°F). If the dry yeast is combined with some of the dry ingredients, the liquid should be very warm (120°F to 130°F). Liquid that is too hot will kill the yeast; liquid that is too cool won't activate the yeast.

- Add flour gradually during kneading. The secret is to add just enough flour to keep the dough from being sticky.

- Place dough in a warm, draft-free place to rise. A temperature of between 80°F and 85°F is best for rising. If your kitchen is cool, place the bowl containing the dough on the top rack of an unheated oven and place a bowl filled with hot water on the rack beneath it.

- Test the dough to be sure it has risen enough by lightly pressing two fingers about ½ inch into the center. If the indentations remain, the dough has risen sufficiently.

TECHNIQUE: KNEADING

Knead dough on lightly floured surface.

1. Place heels of both hands in center of dough; push dough forward as far as possible.
2. Fold dough in half.
3. Pick up folded dough and turn it a quarter turn.

Repeat steps 1, 2 and 3 until dough is smooth and elastic, about 4 to 10 minutes.

DESSERTS

Easy Apple Custard Pie,
page 50

FRESH FRUIT CRISP

 DESSERTS

Filling
- 6 cups peeled, thinly sliced apples, peaches or pears (about 6 to 8 medium)*
- ¼ cup water
- ¼ cup firmly packed brown sugar
- 2 tablespoons all-purpose flour
- ½ teaspoon ground cinnamon

Topping
- 1 cup Quaker® Oats (quick or old fashioned, uncooked)
- ½ cup coarsely chopped walnuts, pecans or almonds (optional)
- ¼ cup firmly packed brown sugar
- ¼ cup (½ stick) margarine or butter, melted
- ¼ teaspoon ground cinnamon

Vanilla ice cream or whipped cream (optional)

See page 50 for recommended baking apples and page 37 for recommended baking pears.

1 Heat oven to 350°F. In large bowl, combine fruit and water. Add sugar, flour and cinnamon; stir until fruit is evenly coated. Spoon into 8-inch square baking dish.

2 Combine topping ingredients; mix well. Sprinkle evenly over fruit.

3 Bake 30 to 35 minutes or until fruit is tender. Serve warm with ice cream or whipped cream, if desired.

Yield: 9 servings

CHERRY NECTARINE CRISPS

Filling

- 3 cups unpeeled, thinly sliced nectarines (about 3 medium)
- 1 cup pitted, quartered sweet cherries (about 25 to 30)
- ½ cup orange juice
- 2 tablespoons firmly packed brown sugar
- 1 tablespoon all-purpose flour

Topping

- ¾ cup Quaker® Oats (quick or old fashioned, uncooked)
- 3 tablespoons firmly packed brown sugar
- 3 tablespoons margarine or butter, melted
- 2 tablespoons all-purpose flour
- ¼ teaspoon ground cinnamon

1 Heat oven to 350°F. In large bowl, combine fruit, orange juice, sugar and flour; stir until fruit is evenly coated. Spoon into six small (about 6 ounce) ovenproof custard or soufflé cups, dividing evenly.

2 Combine topping ingredients; mix well. Sprinkle 2 tablespoons topping over each fruit cup.

3 Bake 20 to 24 minutes or until fruit is tender. Serve warm.

Yield: 6 servings

TEMPTING TOPPERS FOR CRISPS

- A scoop of ice cream or frozen yogurt

- Half-and-half or heavy cream

- Lightly sweetened whipped cream

- Vanilla or fruit-flavored yogurt

- Shredded cheddar or colby cheese (especially good with apple and pear crisps)

LEMON POPPY SEED CAKE

Cake

- 2¼ cups all-purpose flour
- 1½ cups Quaker® Oats (quick or old fashioned, uncooked)
- 3 tablespoons poppy seeds
- 1 tablespoon baking powder
- ½ teaspoon baking soda
- ½ teaspoon salt (optional)
- 1 cup sugar
- ¾ cup (1½ sticks) margarine or butter, softened
- 1 tablespoon grated lemon peel
- 3 eggs
- 1½ cups low-fat milk

Glaze

- 1 cup powdered sugar
- ½ teaspoon grated lemon peel
- 4 to 5 teaspoons fresh lemon juice

1 Heat oven to 350°F. Grease and flour 12-cup Bundt® or 10-inch tube pan.

2 Combine flour, oats, poppy seeds, baking powder, baking soda and salt; set aside.

3 In large bowl, beat sugar and margarine until creamy. Beat in lemon peel. Add eggs one at a time, beating well after each. Beat in dry ingredients and milk alternately in three additions, beginning and ending with dry ingredients. Pour batter into pan.

4 Bake 35 to 45 minutes* or until wooden pick inserted in center comes out clean. Cool 10 minutes; remove from pan. Cool completely on wire rack.

5 Combine powdered sugar, lemon peel and enough lemon juice for desired consistency; mix until smooth. Drizzle over cake. Store tightly covered at room temperature.

Yield: 16 servings

*If using a heavy, cast aluminum Bundt® pan, baking time may need to be increased.

LAZY DAISY OATMEAL CAKE

Cake
- 1¼ cups boiling water
- 1 cup Quaker® Oats (quick or old fashioned, uncooked)
- 1¾ cups all-purpose flour
- 1 teaspoon baking soda
- 1 teaspoon ground cinnamon
- ¼ teaspoon salt (optional)
- ¼ teaspoon ground nutmeg (optional)
- 1 cup granulated sugar
- 1 cup firmly packed brown sugar
- ⅓ cup (5 tablespoons plus 1 teaspoon) margarine or butter, softened
- 2 egg whites or 1 egg
- 1 teaspoon vanilla

Topping
- ½ cup shredded coconut
- ½ cup firmly packed brown sugar
- ½ cup Quaker® Oats (quick or old fashioned, uncooked)
- 3 tablespoons skim milk
- 2 tablespoons margarine or butter, melted

1 Heat oven to 350°F. Lightly grease and flour 8 or 9-inch square baking pan.

2 Combine boiling water and oats; set aside. Combine flour, baking soda, cinnamon, salt and nutmeg; set aside.

3 In large bowl, beat sugars and margarine until creamy. Add egg whites and vanilla; beat well. Add dry ingredients and oat mixture; mix well. Pour batter into pan.

4 Bake 55 to 65 minutes (8-inch square pan) or 50 to 60 minutes (9-inch square pan) or until wooden pick inserted in center comes out clean.

5 Combine topping ingredients; mix well. Spread over top of hot cake. Broil about 4 inches from heat, 1 to 2 minutes or just until topping is bubbly. (Watch carefully; topping burns easily.) Cool on wire rack. Store loosely covered at room temperature.

Yield: 12 servings

GINGER OAT CRUMB CAKE

Topping

1/3	cup Quaker® Oats (quick or old fashioned, uncooked)
1/4	cup all-purpose flour
1/4	cup firmly packed brown sugar
2 to 3	tablespoons finely chopped crystallized ginger or 1 teaspoon ground ginger
3	tablespoons margarine or butter, chilled and cut into pieces

Cake

1¼	cups boiling water
1	cup Quaker® Oats (quick or old fashioned, uncooked)
1¾	cups all-purpose flour
1	tablespoon ground ginger
1	teaspoon baking soda
1	teaspoon ground cinnamon
½	teaspoon ground cloves
¼	teaspoon salt (optional)
1	cup granulated sugar
1	cup firmly packed brown sugar
5	tablespoons margarine or butter, softened
2	egg whites
1	teaspoon vanilla

1 Heat oven to 350°F. Lightly grease and flour 9-inch square or 11 x 7-inch baking pan.

2 Combine oats, flour, sugar and ginger for topping; mix well. Cut in margarine* with pastry blender or two knives until mixture is crumbly; set aside.

3 Combine boiling water and oats; set aside. Combine flour, ginger, baking soda, cinnamon, cloves and salt; set aside. In large bowl, beat sugars and margarine until well blended. Add egg whites and vanilla; beat well. Add dry ingredients and oat mixture; mix just until dry ingredients are moistened. Pour batter into pan. Sprinkle with reserved topping.

4 Bake 50 to 60 minutes or until wooden pick inserted in center comes out clean. Cool on wire rack. Store tightly covered at room temperature.

Yield: 12 servings

*For an explanation of this technique, see page 37.

ALL ABOUT GINGER

- **Fresh Ginger**
  Also called gingerroot, fresh ginger is available in the produce section. Look for ginger that is smooth, firm and plump. Wrapped and refrigerated, fresh ginger will keep about 1 week. To use in baking, remove outer skin with vegetable peeler, then finely chop with a sharp knife.

- **Crystallized Ginger**
  Also called candied ginger, crystallized ginger is peeled, fresh ginger cooked in a sugar syrup then coated with sugar. It is sold packed in jars in the spice section. Store tightly covered at room temperature.

- **Ground Ginger**
  Dried ground gingerroot is sold in jars in the spice section. Store tightly covered in a cool, dry cabinet.

DOUBLE BERRY CAKE

Cake
- 1½ cups all-purpose flour
- ¾ cup Quaker® Oats (quick or old fashioned, uncooked)
- 2 teaspoons baking powder
- ½ teaspoon baking soda
- 1 cup sugar
- ½ cup (1 stick) margarine or butter, softened
- 4 egg whites or 2 eggs
- One 8-ounce container light sour cream
- 1 teaspoon vanilla
- ⅓ cup raspberry preserves
- ¾ cup fresh or frozen blueberries (do not thaw)

Topping
- ½ cup Quaker® Oats (quick or old fashioned, uncooked)
- ¼ cup sugar
- 3 tablespoons margarine or butter, melted
- ¼ teaspoon ground cinnamon

1 Heat oven to 350°F. Lightly grease 9-inch square baking pan.

2 Combine flour, oats, baking powder and baking soda; set aside.

3 In large bowl, beat sugar and margarine until creamy. Add egg whites, sour cream and vanilla; beat well. Add dry ingredients; mix just until dry ingredients are moistened. Spread batter evenly in pan. Spoon preserves over batter; swirl through batter with knife. Sprinkle blueberries evenly over batter.

4 Combine topping ingredients; mix well. Sprinkle over blueberries.

5 Bake 50 to 55 minutes or until wooden pick inserted in center comes out clean. Cool on wire rack. Serve warm. Store loosely covered at room temperature.

Yield: 12 servings

OLD FASHIONED OATMEAL PIE

2 eggs
¾ cup sugar
¾ cup dark corn syrup
¼ cup (½ stick) margarine or butter, melted
2 tablespoons all-purpose flour
1 teaspoon vanilla
¾ cup Quaker® Oats (quick or old fashioned, uncooked)
⅓ cup shredded coconut
One unbaked 9-inch pie crust

Ice cream or whipped cream (optional)

1 Heat oven to 350°F. In large bowl, beat eggs until foamy. Gradually beat in sugar, corn syrup, margarine, flour and vanilla; mix well. Add oats and coconut; mix well. Pour into pie crust.

2 Bake 45 to 55 minutes or until center of pie is set. Cool completely on wire rack.

3 Serve with ice cream or whipped cream, if desired. Store tightly covered in refrigerator.

Yield: 10 servings

PIE CRUST PRIMER

- **Oat Crusts**
  Oat crusts taste very much like an oatmeal cookie. Quick or old fashioned oats are combined with flour, sugar and melted margarine or butter. The mixture is pressed into a pie plate and baked.

- **Crumb Crusts**
  Crumb crusts are similar to oat crusts. Graham crackers, vanilla wafers, chocolate wafers, sandwich cookies, gingersnaps, granola, even pretzels can be used to make a crumb crust.

- **Pastry Crusts**
  Pastry crusts can be made from scratch or purchased as frozen unbaked pie crusts or refrigerated pie crusts. Depending upon the amount of filling in a recipe, it sometimes is necessary to use a *deep dish* frozen pie crust.

EASY APPLE CUSTARD PIE

Crust

- 1¼ cups all-purpose flour
- ¾ cup Quaker® Oats (quick or old fashioned, uncooked)
- ¼ cup firmly packed brown sugar
- ⅛ teaspoon salt (optional)
- ½ cup (1 stick) margarine or butter, melted
- 1 tablespoon water
- 1 teaspoon vanilla

Filling

- One 8-ounce container light sour cream
- ⅔ cup firmly packed brown sugar
- ¼ cup all-purpose flour
- 2 eggs or 4 egg whites, lightly beaten
- ½ teaspoon ground cinnamon
- ⅛ teaspoon ground nutmeg
- 4 cups peeled, thinly sliced apples (about 4 to 5 medium)

Topping

- ¼ cup Quaker® Oats (quick or old fashioned, uncooked)
- ¼ cup firmly packed brown sugar
- ¼ cup all-purpose flour
- ¼ cup (½ stick) margarine or butter, chilled and cut into pieces

TIP · Their tart flavor and firm texture make these apple varieties best for baking: Jonathan, McIntosh, Winesap, Granny Smith, Northern Spy, Greening and Rome Beauty. One medium apple equals about 1 cup sliced or chopped apples.

1 Heat oven to 375°F. For crust, combine dry ingredients in medium bowl; mix well. Add margarine, water and vanilla; mix well. Press firmly onto bottom and sides of 9-inch pie plate, forming a ¼-inch rim around edge. Bake 12 to 15 minutes or until light golden brown. Cool on wire rack.

2 For filling, combine sour cream, sugar, flour, eggs, cinnamon and nutmeg in large bowl; mix well. Add apples; mix well. Spoon filling into cooled crust.

3 For topping, combine oats, sugar and flour in medium bowl; cut in margarine* with pastry blender or two knives until mixture is crumbly. Sprinkle evenly over filling.

4 Bake 50 to 60 minutes or until knife inserted in center comes out clean. Serve warm or chilled. Store tightly covered in refrigerator.

Yield: 8 servings

*For an explanation of this technique, see page 37.

CLASSIC AMERICAN FRUIT DESSERTS

- **Brown Betty:** Fruit, usually apples, combined with sugar and spices, topped with buttered bread crumbs and baked.

- **Buckle:** A cousin of the coffeecake. Fresh fruit is folded into a simple cake batter, covered with a crumbly topping and baked.

- **Cobbler:** Sweetened fruit covered with a biscuit-like crust and baked. The dough originally was dropped on top of the fruit in clumps, giving the crust a cobbled appearance.

- **Crisp:** Sweetened fruit covered with a crumbly topping often containing oats in addition to butter, flour and sugar and baked.

- **Crumble:** A baked fruit pudding with British origins that is similar to a brown betty but with a crumbly oat pastry.

- **Grunt:** Similar to a cobbler, this fruit pudding is cooked in a skillet on the stove top rather than in the oven.

- **Pandowdy:** Traditionally made with sliced apples or peaches sweetened with brown sugar or molasses, the fruit is topped with a biscuit-like batter that becomes crisp during baking.

NOT-SO-SINFUL SUNDAE PIE

1	cup Quaker® Oats (quick or old fashioned, uncooked)
½	cup all-purpose flour
⅓	cup (5 tablespoons plus 1 teaspoon) margarine or butter, melted
¼	cup firmly packed brown sugar
One	quart fat-free or low-fat vanilla frozen yogurt, softened
2	cups any combination fresh fruit, such as blueberries, halved strawberries or sliced bananas
	Fat-free hot fudge topping or berry-flavored fruit syrup (optional)

TIP· Before cutting frozen yogurt and ice cream pies, let pie stand at room temperature 10 to 15 minutes. Use a thin, sharp knife; dip knife in hot water and wipe dry with paper towel between each cut.

1 Heat oven to 350°F. Lightly grease 9-inch pie plate.

2 Combine oats, flour, margarine and sugar; mix well. Press firmly onto bottom and sides of pie plate. Bake 18 to 20 minutes or until golden brown. Cool completely on wire rack.

3 Spoon softened yogurt into cooled crust, spreading evenly. Cover and freeze until firm, about 5 hours.

4 Remove pie from freezer 10 to 15 minutes before serving. Cut into wedges. Top with fruit. Serve with toppings, if desired. Store tightly covered in freezer.

Yield: 8 servings

Pumpkin Silk Pie

Crust

- 1 cup Quaker® Oats (quick or old fashioned, uncooked)
- ¾ cup all-purpose flour
- ½ cup (1 stick) margarine or butter, melted
- ¼ cup firmly packed brown sugar

Filling

- Two 8-ounce packages light cream cheese, softened
- One 16-ounce can pumpkin (1¾ cups)
- 1½ cups powdered sugar
- 2 teaspoons ground cinnamon
- 2 teaspoons vanilla
- ½ teaspoon ground ginger
- ½ teaspoon ground nutmeg
- 2 cups thawed light frozen whipped topping

Light frozen whipped topping, thawed (optional)

Pecan halves (optional)

1 Heat oven to 375°F. Lightly grease 9-inch pie plate.

2 Combine crust ingredients; mix well. Press firmly onto bottom and sides of pie plate. Bake 12 to 15 minutes or until golden brown. Cool completely on wire rack.

3 In large bowl, beat cream cheese, pumpkin, sugar, cinnamon, vanilla, ginger and nutmeg on medium speed of electric mixer until smooth, about 1 to 2 minutes. By hand, gently fold in whipped topping. Spoon filling into cooled crust. Cover and chill 3 hours or overnight.

4 Cut pie into wedges. Top with whipped topping and pecans, if desired. Store tightly covered in refrigerator.

Yield: 10 servings

TECHNIQUE: To fold a lighter ingredient such as whipped topping into a heavier mixture, slide a rubber scraper across bottom of bowl, bringing up the batter on the side of bowl and gently folding it over the top. After each fold, turn bowl slightly. Continue folding and turning bowl until evenly blended.

PUMPKIN POINTERS

- **Check The Label**
  There are two types of canned pumpkin. *Canned pumpkin* is unseasoned pumpkin purée. It is used in most recipes and may be found either with the baking ingredients or canned vegetables. *Canned pumpkin pie filling* contains sugar and spices in addition to the pumpkin purée. It cannot be substituted for canned pumpkin.

- **Storing Canned Pumpkin**
  Leftover canned pumpkin can be transferred to a covered container and stored in the refrigerator up to 1 week. To freeze, transfer to a freezer-safe container; label and freeze up to 6 months. Thaw in refrigerator before using.

MOCHA CHIP CHEESECAKE BARS

Crust

- ½ cup (1 stick) margarine or butter, softened
- ½ cup firmly packed brown sugar
- 1¼ cups Quaker® Oats (quick or old fashioned, uncooked)
- 1 cup all-purpose flour

Filling

- Three 8-ounce packages regular or light cream cheese, softened
- ¾ cup granulated sugar
- 2 tablespoons instant coffee granules or espresso powder
- 1 tablespoon unsweetened cocoa powder
- 1 teaspoon vanilla
- 3 eggs
- 1 cup mini semisweet chocolate pieces, divided

1 Heat oven to 350°F. Beat margarine and sugar until creamy. Add oats and flour; mix well. Press dough onto bottom of ungreased 13 x 9-inch baking pan. Bake 15 minutes. Cool on wire rack.

2 In large bowl, beat cream cheese, sugar, instant coffee, cocoa powder and vanilla on medium speed of electric mixer until smooth. Add eggs; beat just until well blended. Stir in ¾ cup chocolate pieces. Pour filling evenly over crust. Sprinkle with remaining ¼ cup chocolate pieces.

3 Bake 30 to 35 minutes or just until center is set. Cool completely on wire rack. Cut into bars. Store tightly covered in refrigerator.

Yield: 24 bars

PERFECT CHEESECAKES

When making fillings for cheesecake bars and cheesecakes, follow these tips for perfectly delicious results.

- Use either regular or light cream cheese in bricks to make the recipes in this book. Do not substitute soft cream cheese in tubs.

- Let cream cheese stand at room temperature until softened or follow the directions on the package for microwave softening. Cream cheese that is too cold will form small lumps in the batter.

- After adding eggs to batter, beat just until well blended.

- To test for doneness, grasp sides of pan with oven mitts and gently move pan. If center of filling jiggles, remove from oven to rack. During cooling, the center continues cooking and becomes firm.

1 cup (2 sticks) margarine or butter, softened
½ cup firmly packed brown sugar
1½ cups Quaker® Oats (quick or old fashioned, uncooked)
¾ cup all-purpose flour
½ cup chopped walnuts, pecans or almonds
¾ teaspoon ground cinnamon
½ teaspoon baking soda
2⅔ cups shredded coconut, toasted, divided
Two 8-ounce containers lemon nonfat or low-fat yogurt
One 8-ounce container light frozen whipped topping, thawed
2 teaspoons grated lemon peel

Lemon twists (optional)

TIP· To toast coconut, arrange in even layer in 13 x 9-inch baking pan. Bake at 350° F for 18 to 20 minutes or until coconut is lightly toasted, stirring after 12 minutes. Cool completely.

1 Heat oven to 350°F. In large bowl, beat margarine and brown sugar until creamy. Add oats, flour, walnuts, cinnamon and baking soda; mix well. Add 1 cup toasted coconut; mix well. Press dough onto bottom of ungreased 13 x 9-inch baking pan. Bake 18 to 20 minutes or until golden brown. Cool completely on wire rack.

2 In large bowl, combine yogurt, whipped topping and lemon peel. Spread evenly over cooled crust. Sprinkle with remaining 1⅔ cups coconut, patting gently. Cover and chill several hours or overnight.

3 Cut into squares and garnish with lemon twists, if desired. Store tightly covered in refrigerator.

Yield: 15 servings

1992 Grand Prize
Carole MacKenzie, Santa Barbara, CA

MAIN DISHES

*Sunday Supper
Meatloaf, page 58*

Total preparation and cooking time: 1¼ hours

1½	**pounds ground turkey breast**
One	**10-ounce package frozen chopped spinach, thawed and drained**
1	**cup Quaker® Oats (quick or old fashioned, uncooked)**
½	**cup finely chopped onion**
½	**cup shredded carrots**
2	**egg whites or 1 egg, lightly beaten**
⅓	**cup skim milk**
1½	**teaspoons Italian seasoning**
1	**teaspoon salt (optional)**
¼	**teaspoon black pepper**

TIP · Lean ground beef may be substituted for ground turkey breast. Bake 50 to 55 minutes or until thermometer registers 160°F and center is no longer pink.

VARIATION: Substitute ½ cup finely chopped green or red bell pepper for spinach.

1 Heat oven to 350°F. In large bowl, combine all ingredients; mix lightly but thoroughly. Shape turkey mixture into 9 x 5-inch loaf in 13 x 9-inch baking pan or on rack of broiler pan.

2 Bake 1 hour or until thermometer registers 170°F and center is no longer pink. Let turkey loaf stand about 5 minutes before slicing.

Yield: 8 servings

THE PERFECT MEATLOAF

- A meatloaf made with oats has a soft, moist texture, and oats are more convenient to use than fresh bread crumbs.

- Use a gentle touch when mixing; overmixing can cause meatloaf to be firm and compact after cooking.

- Bake meatloaf to medium doneness (160°F) or until no longer pink.* Overcooking causes meatloaf to be dry.

- For easier slicing, allow meatloaf to stand a few minutes before cutting.

*Meatloaves made with ground turkey should be cooked to 170°F.

SUNDAY SUPPER MEATLOAF

Total preparation and cooking time: 1½ hours

Roasted Vegetables
- 2 tablespoons olive oil
- 2 cloves garlic, minced
- ¾ teaspoon dried thyme leaves
- ½ teaspoon salt (optional)
- ¼ teaspoon black pepper
- 1½ pounds medium red potatoes, quartered
- 1 pound carrots, cut diagonally into ¾-inch pieces
- 1 small yellow onion, cut lengthwise into ½-inch wedges

Meatloaf
- 1½ pounds lean ground beef
- ¾ cup Quaker® Oats (quick or old fashioned, uncooked)
- ¾ cup finely chopped onion
- ½ cup chili sauce or catsup
- 1 egg, lightly beaten
- 1 tablespoon Worcestershire sauce
- 2 cloves garlic, minced
- 1 teaspoon dried thyme leaves
- ¾ teaspoon black pepper
- ½ teaspoon salt (optional)

1 Heat oven to 350°F. For vegetables, combine oil, garlic, thyme, salt and pepper in large bowl. Add vegetables; toss to coat. Transfer to 15 x 10-inch jelly roll pan, spreading evenly; set aside.

2 For meatloaf, combine all ingredients in large bowl; mix lightly but thoroughly. Shape meatloaf mixture into 8 x 4-inch loaf on rack of broiler pan.

3 Place meatloaf on upper oven rack; place vegetables on rack below. Bake 50 to 55 minutes or until meatloaf is to medium doneness (160°F) and vegetables are tender. Brush with additional chili sauce during last 10 minutes of baking, if desired.

4 Cut meatloaf into 6 slices; serve with vegetables.

Yield: 6 servings

PRIZE-WINNING MEATLOAF

Total preparation and cooking time: 1¼ hours

1½ pounds lean ground beef
1 cup tomato juice or tomato sauce
¾ cup Quaker® Oats (quick or old fashioned, uncooked)
1 egg or 2 egg whites, lightly beaten
¼ cup chopped onion
½ teaspoon salt (optional)
¼ teaspoon black pepper

VARIATIONS: Customize meatloaf by adding *one* of the following to meatloaf ingredients:
• ½ cup frozen (thawed) or canned (drained) corn
• ½ cup chopped green or red bell pepper
• One 2½-ounce jar sliced mushrooms, drained
• ⅓ cup grated Parmesan cheese
• 2 tablespoons finely chopped parsley or cilantro

TOPPINGS (OPTIONAL):
• Sprinkle top of baked meatloaf with 1 cup shredded cheese.
• Spoon prepared spaghetti sauce, pizza sauce, barbecue sauce or salsa over each serving.

1 Heat oven to 350°F. In large bowl, combine all ingredients; mix lightly but thoroughly. Press meatloaf mixture into 8 x 4-inch loaf pan.

2 Bake 1 hour or until meatloaf is to medium doneness (160°F) and center is no longer pink. Let meatloaf stand 5 minutes; drain off any juices before slicing.

Yield: 8 servings

MINI TEX-MEX MEATLOAVES

EASY ACCOMPANIMENTS

Try one of these easy accompaniments with any of the meatloaf recipes in this chapter.

- Couscous, rice or orzo (a small rice-shaped pasta) prepared according to package directions. Stir in shredded carrots, thinly sliced green onions or frozen peas (thawed) just before serving.

- Frozen vegetable blend prepared according to package directions.

- Frozen thick-cut potato wedges baked according to package directions. Sprinkle with garlic salt or grated Parmesan cheese.

- Packaged scalloped or au gratin potatoes prepared according to package directions.

Total preparation and cooking time: 30 minutes

1½ pounds lean ground beef
¾ cup Quaker® Oats (quick or old fashioned, uncooked)
½ cup mild chunky salsa
¼ cup chopped cilantro
1 egg, lightly beaten
2 teaspoons chili powder
1½ teaspoons ground cumin
½ teaspoon salt (optional)

¾ cup mild chunky salsa
¾ cup (3 ounces) shredded cheddar cheese

1 Heat oven to 400°F. In large bowl, combine all ingredients except ¾ cup salsa and cheese; mix lightly but thoroughly. Press approximately ⅓ cup meatloaf mixture into each of 12 medium muffin cups.

2 Bake 15 to 20 minutes or until centers are no longer pink.

3 Remove meatloaves from oven. Top each with 1 tablespoon salsa; sprinkle each with 1 tablespoon cheese. Bake 3 minutes or until cheese is melted. Remove meatloaves from pan and serve.

Yield: 6 servings

Total preparation and cooking time: 30 minutes

Salsa

  1 cup mild or medium chunky salsa
  1 medium-size ripe mango, peeled and cubed (about 1 cup)
  2 tablespoons coarsely chopped cilantro (optional)

Meatballs

  1 pound lean ground beef
  ¾ cup Quaker® Oats (quick or old fashioned, uncooked)
  ¾ cup finely chopped red onion
  ¼ cup skim milk
  1 clove garlic, minced
1½ tablespoons coarsely chopped cilantro
  1 teaspoon dried oregano leaves
  ¾ teaspoon salt (optional)
  ½ teaspoon ground cumin

  6 (6 inch) corn or flour tortillas, warmed

VARIATION: Substitute 1 cup peeled, diced peaches or pineapple for mango.

1 In medium bowl, combine all salsa ingredients; mix well. Set aside.

2 In large bowl, combine all meatball ingredients; mix lightly but thoroughly. Shape into eighteen 1½-inch meatballs; arrange on 6 metal skewers.

3 Broil meatballs 4 to 5 inches from heat source 5 to 8 minutes per side or until centers are no longer pink.

4 Remove meatballs from skewers; serve with salsa and tortillas.

Yield: 6 servings

TIP · To warm tortillas, stack between microwave-safe paper towels. Microwave on HIGH 15 to 30 seconds or until warm.

FACTS ABOUT MANGOES

- Mangoes are available year-round, but their peak season is May through September. When fully ripe, the skin of a mango will be yellow with a red blush; the flesh will be a brilliant orange, sweet and juicy.

- To ripen a mango, place in a paper bag at room temperature. Ripe mangoes may be placed in the crisper drawer or a plastic bag and refrigerated for several days.

- To dice a mango, first remove the skin with a sharp knife. Carefully cut the flesh away from the large flat seed that runs the length of the fruit and cut into pieces.

- Dried mango can be found in larger supermarkets. It must be soaked in water before being used.

DILLED SALMON CAKES

Total preparation and cooking time: 30 minutes

Sauce
- ½ **cup plain nonfat yogurt**
- ⅓ **cup seeded, chopped tomato**
- ⅓ **cup seeded, chopped cucumber**
- 1 **tablespoon finely chopped onion**
- 1 **tablespoon finely chopped fresh dill or 1 teaspoon dried dill weed**

Salmon Cakes
- One **14¾-ounce can pink salmon, drained, skin and bones removed**
- ¾ **cup Quaker® Oats (quick or old fashioned, uncooked)**
- ⅓ **cup skim milk**
- 2 **egg whites, lightly beaten**
- 2 **tablespoons finely chopped onion**
- 1 **tablespoon finely chopped fresh dill or 1 teaspoon dried dill weed**
- ¼ **teaspoon salt (optional)**

1 In small bowl, combine sauce ingredients; mix well. Cover and chill.

2 In medium bowl, combine salmon cake ingredients; mix well. Let stand 5 minutes. Shape into 5 oval patties about 1 inch thick.

3 Lightly spray non-stick skillet with no-stick cooking spray. Cook salmon cakes over medium heat 3 to 4 minutes on each side or until golden brown and heated through. Serve with sauce.

Yield: 5 servings

GARDEN PIZZAS

Total preparation and cooking time: 1 hour

⅔ cup warm water (105˚F – 115˚F)

One ¼-ounce package (about 2¼ teaspoons) quick-rising yeast

1 tablespoon olive oil

2 teaspoons sugar

1⅓ cups all-purpose flour

¾ cup Quaker® Oats (quick or old fashioned, uncooked)

¼ cup shredded or grated Parmesan cheese

1½ cups (6 ounces) shredded part-skim mozzarella cheese, divided

½ cup thinly sliced green bell pepper

½ cup thinly sliced red onion

¼ cup chopped fresh basil or 4 teaspoons dried basil leaves

2 cloves garlic, minced

4 plum tomatoes, thinly sliced (about 2 cups)

TIP· Pizzas may be grilled. After shaping crusts, grill over medium-hot coals 2 to 4 minutes or until bottoms are golden brown. Remove from grill. On browned side of crusts, layer toppings as directed below. Return to grill. Cover; grill 4 to 6 minutes or until bottoms are golden brown and cheese begins to melt.

1 In small bowl, combine water, yeast, oil and sugar; let stand 10 minutes or until foamy.

2 In large bowl, combine flour and oats. Add yeast mixture and blend on low speed of electric mixer until moistened. Beat 2 minutes at medium speed.

3 Turn dough out onto lightly floured surface. Knead 1 minute. Shape dough into ball; place in greased bowl, turning once. Cover; let rise in warm place 20 minutes or until nearly doubled in size.

4 Heat oven to 425˚F. Spray cookie sheet with no-stick cooking spray or oil lightly.

5 Punch dough down; divide into four portions. On cookie sheet, pat each portion of dough into 6-inch circle. Top with Parmesan cheese, ¾ cup mozzarella cheese, bell pepper, onion, basil, garlic and tomatoes, dividing evenly. Sprinkle with remaining ¾ cup mozzarella cheese.

6 Bake 20 minutes or until crust is golden brown.

Yield: 4 individual pizzas

BREAKFASTS

See Tasty Toppers, pages 69 and 70

A HEALTHY START FOR A HEALTHY HEART

Mom was right!

Eating oatmeal *is* a wholesome way to start the day. Not only does a bowl of hot oatmeal warm you up and keep you feeling satisfied all morning long, eating oatmeal daily may help reduce the risk of heart disease when it's part of a diet that's low in saturated fat and cholesterol.

Numerous studies at leading universities have shown that the soluble fiber found in oats is what is responsible for helping to reduce blood cholesterol levels. Oat soluble fiber helps control blood cholesterol by binding some of the cholesterol in your digestive tract. This cholesterol is eliminated from your body naturally.

How much oatmeal is needed to positively affect cholesterol levels? One large bowl of oatmeal (about a serving and a half) should result in a reduction of blood cholesterol for most people. To make 1½ servings (or 1½ cups of cooked oatmeal), use ¾ cup oats (quick or old fashioned) and 1½ cups water; cook for the time given on the package.

Featured in this chapter are several recipes for hot oatmeal as well as a cool and creamy peach and berry muesli, delicious whole grain oatmeal pancakes, and a crunchy granola sweetened with honey and chock-full of dried fruit. They're all easy to make and a delicious way to start the day.

TIP

Increasing the amount of oatmeal in your diet is easier than you might think. To get you started . . .

- **Begin the day with a bowl of hot oatmeal or a low-fat oatmeal muffin.**

- **Use oatmeal in place of bread crumbs in recipes for meatloaf and meatballs.**

- **Snack on oatmeal ready-to-eat cereals like Quaker® Toasted Oatmeal and Quaker® Oatmeal Squares and low-fat oatmeal raisin cookies.**

- **Substitute ⅓ cup oats for ⅓ cup flour whenever you bake.**

- **Coat skinned chicken breasts and fish fillets with ground oat flour instead of bread or cracker crumbs.**

IN A HURRY?

Quick and Old Fashioned Quaker®
Oats can be cooked in the microwave
oven. Simply follow the easy microwave directions on the package. For
extra convenience, try a pouch of
either Quaker® Quick 'n Hearty™
Microwave Oatmeal or Instant
Quaker® Oatmeal. Both are available
in regular and a variety of flavors.

DID YOU KNOW?

January is National Oatmeal Month because
we buy more oatmeal during that month than
any other month. In January 1996, Americans
bought more than 20 million pounds of
Quaker oatmeal.

FIBER FACTS

*Soluble and insoluble fibers are
the two types of dietary fiber
important for good health.*

Fiber x 2

*One serving (½ cup uncooked) of Quick or Old
Fashioned Quaker® Oats contains **two** grams of
soluble fiber and **two** grams of insoluble fiber.*

Soluble fibers include pectin,
which is found in apples, and
gums, such as beta glucan, which
are found in oats and barley. Oat
soluble fiber helps control blood
cholesterol levels by binding some
of the cholesterol in the digestive
tract. This cholesterol is eliminated
from the body naturally.

Insoluble fibers are found in foods
such as vegetables, wheat bran,
oats and other whole grains. They
are not absorbed by the body and
help promote regularity. Oats (old
fashioned, quick and instant oatmeal) contain *both* soluble and
insoluble fiber.

FRUIT & HONEY GRANOLA

3½ cups Quaker® Oats (quick or old fashioned, uncooked)
½ cup honey
⅓ cup coarsely chopped pecans (optional)
¼ cup (½ stick) margarine or butter, melted
1 teaspoon vanilla
½ teaspoon ground cinnamon
⅛ to ¼ teaspoon salt (optional)
One 6-ounce package diced dried mixed fruit (about 1⅓ cups)

VARIATION: Substitute dried cranberries, cherries, blueberries or chopped apricots for dried mixed fruit.

TIP· Homemade granola makes a terrific gift. Spoon cooled granola into airtight glass or plastic jars, canisters or cellophane gift bags (tie closed with ribbon). Add a gift tag and be sure to include a copy of the recipe.

1 Heat oven to 350°F. In large bowl, combine all ingredients except dried fruit; mix well. Spread evenly in 15 x 10-inch jelly roll pan.

2 Bake 30 to 35 minutes or until golden brown, stirring every 10 minutes. Cool completely.

3 Stir in dried fruit. Store tightly covered at room temperature up to 1 week.

Yield: 5½ cups

PEACH MUESLI WITH BERRIES

2 cups Quaker® Oats (quick or old fashioned, uncooked)

1½ cups apple juice

1⅓ cups coarsely chopped frozen (thawed) or peeled fresh peaches (about 3 medium)

One 8-ounce container vanilla low-fat yogurt

¼ teaspoon ground nutmeg

Fresh or frozen (thawed) blueberries or raspberries, as desired

TIP · To peel fresh peaches easily, dip in boiling water about 30 seconds; remove with slotted spoon to bowl filled with ice water. Remove skin with small, sharp knife.

VARIATION: Substitute orange juice, apricot nectar or a juice blend for the apple juice.

1 In large bowl, combine all ingredients except berries; mix well. Cover and refrigerate 8 hours or up to 4 days.

2 Serve muesli cold topped with berries.

Yield: 4 servings

2 cups apple juice
1½ cups water
⅓ cup maple-flavored syrup
½ teaspoon ground cinnamon
¼ teaspoon salt (optional)
2 cups Quaker® Oats (quick or old fashioned, uncooked)
1 cup unpeeled, chopped apple or dried apple pieces
½ cup chopped walnuts or pecans (optional)

1 In medium saucepan, bring juice, water, syrup, cinnamon and salt to a boil; stir in oats and apple.

2 Return to a boil; reduce heat to medium. Cook 1 minute for quick oats or 5 minutes for old fashioned oats or until most of liquid is absorbed, stirring occasionally.

3 Stir in walnuts, if desired. Let stand until desired consistency.

Yield: 4 servings

Microwave Directions: In 3-quart microwaveable bowl, combine all ingredients except nuts. Microwave on HIGH 6 to 7 minutes for quick oats and 9 to 10 minutes for old fashioned oats or until most of liquid is absorbed. Stir in nuts, if desired. Let stand until desired consistency.

Maple Apple Oatmeal pictured on page 71.

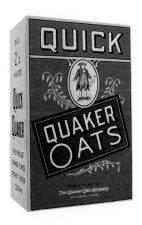

TASTY OATMEAL TOPPERS

Any one of these tasty toppers will add pizzazz—and great taste—to a bowl of hot oatmeal.

• Berries, brown sugar and low-fat milk

• Sliced bananas, ground cinnamon and vanilla low-fat yogurt

• Raisins, ground cinnamon and chopped toasted nuts

• Applesauce and ground cinnamon

• Diced peaches and a dash of ground ginger

• Chopped dates, walnuts and ground nutmeg

• Diced apples, brown sugar and ground cinnamon

• Chopped pears and dried cranberries

BAKED BREAKFAST OATMEAL

MORE TASTY OATMEAL TOPPERS

- Apple-cinnamon low-fat yogurt and diced dried mixed fruit

- Maple-flavored syrup, chopped dates and walnuts

- Raspberry low-fat yogurt and dried cranberries

- Diced dried apricots and honey

- Crushed pineapple, sliced bananas and chopped macadamia nuts

- Blueberry spreadable fruit and toasted wheat germ

Historically speaking, oatmeal puddings have been enjoyed since ancient times. This breakfast pudding is made extra-special by the addition of dried fruit and cinnamon.

2¼ cups Quick Quaker® Oats or 2¾ cups Old
      Fashioned Quaker® Oats (uncooked)
 ¾ cup firmly packed brown sugar
 ¾ cup raisins, dried cranberries or dried cherries
  1 teaspoon ground cinnamon
 ½ teaspoon salt (optional)
3⅓ cups skim milk
  4 egg whites, beaten until foamy
      or ½ cup egg substitute
  1 tablespoon vegetable oil
  1 tablespoon vanilla

     Skim milk or nonfat yogurt and fruit (optional)

1 Heat oven to 350°F. Spray 8-inch square baking dish with no-stick cooking spray.

2 In large bowl, combine oats, sugar, raisins, cinnamon and salt; mix well. Add combined milk, egg whites, oil and vanilla; mix well. Pour into baking dish.

3 Bake 55 to 60 minutes or until center is set and firm to the touch. Cool slightly.

4 Serve topped with milk or yogurt and fruit, if desired. Store leftover oatmeal tightly covered in refrigerator.

Yield: 8 servings

Orange Banana Date Oatmeal

2 cups orange juice

1 cup water

¼ teaspoon salt (optional)

⅛ teaspoon ground nutmeg

1½ cups Quaker® Oats (quick or old fashioned, uncooked)

¾ cup chopped dates or raisins

1 medium-size ripe banana, mashed

1 In medium saucepan, bring juice, water, salt and nutmeg to a boil; stir in oats and dates.

2 Return to a boil; reduce heat to medium. Cook 1 minute for quick oats or 5 minutes for old fashioned oats or until most of liquid is absorbed, stirring occasionally.

3 Stir in banana. Let stand until desired consistency.

Yield: 4 servings

Microwave Directions: In 3-quart microwaveable bowl, combine all ingredients except banana. Microwave on HIGH 6 to 7 minutes for quick oats and 9 to 10 minutes for old fashioned oats or until most of liquid is absorbed. Stir in banana. Let stand until desired consistency.

Also shown: *Maple Apple Oatmeal* (bottom), p. 69

FAVORITE OATMEAL PANCAKES

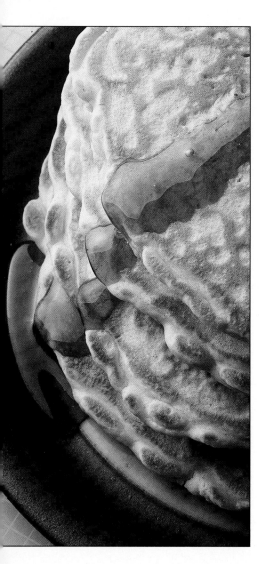

Pancakes

1¼ **cups all-purpose flour**

½ **cup Quaker® Oats (quick or old fashioned, uncooked)**

2 **teaspoons baking powder**

¼ **teaspoon salt (optional)**

1¼ **cups skim milk**

1 **egg, lightly beaten**

1 **tablespoon vegetable oil**

Stir-Ins (optional)

• **1 cup fresh or frozen blueberries (do not thaw)**

• **1 medium-size ripe banana, mashed, and ⅛ teaspoon ground nutmeg**

• **¾ cup finely chopped apple, ¼ cup chopped walnuts or pecans and ½ teaspoon ground cinnamon**

TIP · To keep cooked pancakes warm, arrange on heatproof plate or cookie sheet, cover loosely with aluminum foil and place in 250°F oven.

1 In medium bowl, combine flour, oats, baking powder and salt; mix well. In small bowl, combine milk, egg and oil; blend well. Add to dry ingredients all at once; mix just until dry ingredients are moistened. (Do not overmix.)

2 Add *one* of the stir-in options, if desired.

3 Heat skillet over medium-high heat (or preheat electric skillet or griddle to 375°F). Lightly grease skillet. For each pancake, pour ¼ cup batter into hot skillet. Turn pancakes when tops are covered with bubbles and edges look cooked. Serve hot with favorite topping.

Yield: 12 (4-inch) pancakes

*Valentine Cookie
Puzzle, page 76*

GO BANANAS COOKIE SUNDAES

1 cup (2 sticks) margarine or butter, softened
1 cup firmly packed brown sugar
1½ cups mashed ripe bananas (about 4 medium)
2 eggs
2 teaspoons vanilla
2½ cups Quaker® Oats (quick or old fashioned, uncooked)
2 cups all-purpose flour
1 teaspoon baking soda
¼ teaspoon salt (optional)
1 cup (6 ounces) semisweet chocolate pieces

Ice cream or frozen yogurt, any flavor
Ice cream topping, any flavor

VARIATION: Substitute peanut butter pieces or candy-coated chocolate pieces for the semisweet chocolate pieces.

1 Heat oven to 350°F. Beat margarine and sugar until creamy. Add bananas, eggs and vanilla; beat well. Add combined oats, flour, baking soda and salt; mix well. Stir in chocolate pieces; mix well.

2 Drop dough by ¼ cupfuls 4 inches apart on ungreased cookie sheets; spread to 3½-inch diameter.

3 Bake 14 to 16 minutes or until edges are light golden brown. Cool 1 minute on cookie sheets; remove to wire rack. Cool completely.

4 To serve, top each cookie with a scoop of ice cream; drizzle with ice cream topping. Store leftover cookies tightly covered.

Yield: About 2 dozen

½ cup (1 stick) margarine or butter, softened
½ cup sugar
1 egg
1 teaspoon vanilla
1 cup all-purpose flour
1 cup Quaker® Oats (quick or old fashioned, uncooked)
¼ teaspoon baking soda
¼ teaspoon salt (optional)

Ready-to-spread frosting
Assorted small candies

1 Heat oven to 350°F. Lightly grease large cookie sheet.

2 Beat margarine and sugar until creamy. Add egg and vanilla; beat well. Add combined flour, oats, baking soda and salt; mix well.

3 Spread dough into 10-inch circle about ½ inch thick on cookie sheet.

4 Bake 22 to 25 minutes or until light golden brown. Cool 5 minutes on cookie sheet; carefully loosen with spatula. Remove to wire rack; cool completely.

5 Spread frosting over surface of cookie; gently press candies into frosting. To serve, cut into wedges. Store leftover wedges tightly covered.

Yield: 12 servings

TIP · To make this cookie look like a pizza, tint ready-to-spread vanilla frosting with red and yellow food coloring to resemble pizza sauce. Top with shredded coconut, black jelly beans, strawberry or cherry fruit roll-ups cut into circles and green gummy worms. Melt vanilla milk chips according to package directions and drizzle on top.

CELEBRATION IDEAS

All of life's events, big and small, deserve to be celebrated. The next time there's a reason to celebrate, be ready with one of these treats.

- **Birthday Breakfast**
  Favorite Oatmeal Pancakes, p. 72

- **Family Reunion**
  Caramel Oatmeal Chewies, p. 22

- **Picnic In The Park**
  Oatmeal Dream Dates, p. 24

- **First Day Of Spring**
  Lemon Poppy Seed Cake, p. 45

- **Baby or Bridal Shower**
  Lemon Wafers, p. 18

- **Back-To-School**
  Chewy Oatmeal Spice Cookies, p. 11
  Peanutty Crisscrosses, p. 20
  Cocoa Banana Mini Cakes, p. 85

- **A GREAT Report Card**
  Chewy Choc-Oat-Chip™ Cookies, p. 10

VALENTINE COOKIE PUZZLE

1 cup (2 sticks) margarine or butter, softened
½ cup sugar
1 teaspoon vanilla
2 cups Quaker® Oats (quick or old fashioned, uncooked)
1¼ cups all-purpose flour
Assorted small candies

1 Heat oven to 350°F. Lightly grease two cookie sheets.

2 Beat margarine, sugar and vanilla until creamy. Add combined oats and flour; mix well.

3 Divide dough in half. Pat each half into large heart shape about ¼ inch thick on cookie sheet. Gently press candies into dough. With sharp knife, cut through each heart to form 8 to 10 random shapes. (Do not separate.)

4 Bake 18 to 20 minutes or until lightly browned. Carefully cut through pieces again to separate. Cool 5 minutes on cookie sheet. Remove to wire rack; cool completely. Store tightly covered.

Yield: Two 10-inch hearts

TIP· To package this cookie for gift-giving, line a flat, sturdy cardboard gift box with food-safe tissue or waxed paper. Decorate box top with gift wrap, markers or stickers. Carefully arrange cookie "puzzle pieces" in bottom half of box and close with lid.

1 cup (2 sticks) margarine or butter, softened
1 cup sugar
1 egg
2 tablespoons low-fat milk
1 teaspoon vanilla
2½ cups all-purpose flour
1 cup Quaker® Oats (quick or old fashioned, uncooked)
1 teaspoon baking soda
½ teaspoon salt (optional)

Assorted small candies or colored sugars
Egg glaze*

For Egg Glaze: Combine 1 egg yolk and ¼ teaspoon water; divide into three small dishes. Tint each with food coloring. With small brush, paint glaze on cookies as desired. Bake as directed below.

1 Beat margarine and sugar until creamy. Add egg, milk and vanilla; beat well. Add combined flour, oats, baking soda and salt; mix well. Divide dough in half for easier handling. Cover; chill 2 to 3 hours.

2 Heat oven to 350°F. Roll out dough to ⅛ inch thickness on lightly floured surface. Cut with floured 2 to 3-inch cookie cutters. Place 1 inch apart on ungreased cookie sheets. Decorate with candies and colored sugars or brush with egg glaze.

3 Bake 8 to 10 minutes or until edges are light golden brown. Cool 1 minute on cookie sheets; remove to wire rack. Cool completely. Store tightly covered.

Yield: About 4 dozen

Spring-Into-Easter Cutouts pictured on page 78.

PERFECT CUT-OUT COOKIES

- Divide dough into two or three portions before chilling. Roll out one portion at a time, keeping remainder covered and chilled.

- With lightly floured rolling pin, roll out dough on lightly floured surface to an even thickness; start from center and roll to edges.

- Using cookie cutters, cut out shapes as close together as possible. Cookie cutters with simple shapes and sharp edges give the best results.

- Use pancake turner or wide spatula to transfer cookies to cookie sheets.

- Chill dough scraps before rerolling.

CITRUS STREUSEL SQUARES

1½ cups firmly packed brown sugar

1 cup (2 sticks) margarine or butter, softened

2½ cups all-purpose flour

2 cups Quaker® Oats (quick or old fashioned, uncooked)

2 teaspoons baking powder

1 teaspoon salt (optional)

One 14-ounce can sweetened condensed milk (not evaporated milk)

¼ cup lemon juice

¼ cup orange juice

2 teaspoons grated lemon peel

2 teaspoons grated orange peel

Powdered sugar

1 Heat oven to 350°F. Beat brown sugar and margarine until creamy. Add combined flour, oats, baking powder and salt; mix until crumbly. Reserve 2 cups oat mixture for topping; set aside. Press remaining oat mixture onto bottom of ungreased 13 x 9-inch baking pan.

2 Combine condensed milk, lemon juice, orange juice and peels; mix well. Spread mixture evenly over crust. Sprinkle with reserved oat mixture, patting gently.

3 Bake 35 to 40 minutes or until light golden brown. Cool completely.

4 Sprinkle with powdered sugar. Cut into squares. Store tightly covered.

Yield: 30 squares

Also shown: *Spring-Into-Easter Cutouts* (bottom), p. 77

Cookies

- 1 cup (2 sticks) margarine or butter, softened
- ¾ cup firmly packed brown sugar
- ¾ cup granulated sugar
- 1 cup canned pumpkin
- 1 egg
- 1 teaspoon vanilla
- 2½ cups Quaker® Oats (quick or old fashioned, uncooked)
- 1¾ cups all-purpose flour
- 1 teaspoon pumpkin pie spice or ground cinnamon
- 1 teaspoon baking soda
- ¼ teaspoon salt (optional)

Frosting

- 2½ cups powdered sugar
- One 3-ounce package cream cheese, softened
- 1 tablespoon milk
- ½ teaspoon vanilla
- Yellow and red food coloring (optional)

TIP · Look for pumpkin pie spice in the spice section. To make your own, combine 4 teaspoons ground cinnamon, 1 teaspoon ground ginger, ½ teaspoon ground allspice, ½ teaspoon ground cloves and ½ teaspoon ground nutmeg. Store tightly covered in a cool, dry cabinet.

Decorating Idea: Decorate frosted cookies with Halloween candy to look like jack-o'-lanterns.

1 Heat oven to 350°F. Beat margarine and sugars until creamy. Add pumpkin, egg and vanilla; beat well. Add combined oats, flour, pumpkin pie spice, baking soda and salt; mix well.

2 Drop dough by rounded tablespoonfuls onto ungreased cookie sheets.

3 Bake 11 to 13 minutes or until light golden brown. Cool 1 minute on cookie sheets; remove to wire rack. Cool completely.

4 Combine powdered sugar, cream cheese, milk and vanilla in medium bowl; beat until smooth. Tint frosting orange with yellow and red food coloring, if desired. Frost top of each cookie. Store tightly covered in refrigerator.

Yield: About 4 dozen

MORE CELEBRATIONS

- **Mother's Day**
  Lemon Blueberry Oatmeal Muffins, p. 26

- **Father's Day**
  Peanut Butter Cup Cookies, p. 83
  Giant Brownie Ice Cream Sandwich, p. 88

- **4th Of July**
  Double Berry Cake, p. 48
  Blueberry Streusel Bars, p. 21

- **Labor Day**
  Lazy Daisy Oatmeal Cake, p. 46

- **Columbus Day**
  Italian Herbed Oatmeal Focaccia, p. 40

- **Thanksgiving**
  Pumpkin Silk Pie, p. 53
  Easy Apple Custard Pie, p. 50

- **Christmas**
  Cranberry Orange Bread, p. 33
  Festive Eggnog Bread, p. 36
  Chocolate Cookie Bears, p. 86

1 cup (2 sticks) margarine or butter, softened
¾ cup powdered sugar
1 egg
1 teaspoon vanilla
2 cups all-purpose flour
1¼ cups Quaker® Oats (quick or old fashioned, uncooked)
¼ teaspoon salt (optional)

Approximately 48 assorted bite-size candies such as milk chocolate candy kisses, candy-coated chocolate pieces, jelly beans or gumdrops
Colored sugar or candy sprinkles

1 Heat oven to 325°F. Beat margarine and sugar until creamy. Add egg and vanilla; beat well. Add combined flour, oats and salt; mix well.

2 Shape dough into 1-inch balls. Press desired candy piece into center of each ball; shape dough around candy so it is completely hidden. Roll cookies in colored sugar or candy sprinkles until evenly coated. Place 1½ inches apart on ungreased cookie sheets.

3 Bake 14 to 17 minutes or until cookies are set. Remove to wire rack. Cool completely. Store tightly covered.

Yield: About 4 dozen

VARIATION: After shaping dough around candy, bake as directed. Remove to wire rack; cool 5 minutes. Place ¾ cup powdered sugar in resealable plastic bag. Place 3 or 4 cookies at a time in bag; seal bag and shake gently until cookies are evenly coated with sugar. Cool completely.

BAKE-AHEAD GifTS

Simplify your holiday gift-giving by making cookies and breads ahead and freezing them. Just before giving, thaw and package festively. These ideas may help inspire you.

- **Cookie Bundles:** Use crayons, felt tip pens, stickers and stars to decorate plain white paper plates. Place plastic wrap on plates and arrange cookies on top. Wrap with tinted cellophane and tie with ribbon.

- **Bountiful Baskets:** Wrap cookies, muffins and mini quick bread loaves individually in clear plastic wrap. Pack in baskets filled with colorful, crumpled tissue paper; overwrap with colored cellophane and tie with a festive bow.

- **Beautiful Bread Boards:** Place holiday breads on an attractive cutting board or tray with butter or jam spreader. Wrap with cellophane and tie with ribbons.

- **Create-A-Cookie:** Line a basket with a square of holiday fabric and fill with nonperishable cookie ingredients, candy decorations and a cookie cutter. Attach the recipe to the handle with a ribbon.

- **Homemade Gift Boxes:** Cover boxes or coffee cans with decorative paper or twine and line with colored tissue, cellophane or foil. Tuck favorite cookies inside and tie with a plaid ribbon.

- **Kid Creations:** Children can make their own gift bags for friends or someone special. Cut new sponges into holiday shapes such as stars, trees and bells. Dip in tempera paint and sponge onto paper lunch bags. Wrap cookies in plastic wrap, place in bag and tie closed with ribbon. Attach small candy canes or peppermint sticks with additional ribbon.

- **Cookie Care Packages:** Arrange cookies in holiday tins that are airtight. Use waxed paper to separate layers and help cushion. Pack tins in a sturdy cardboard box with foam packing pieces. Seal, address for mailing and mark top and sides of box "fragile."

- **Homemade Holiday Party Favors:** Individually wrap several cookies in festive food-safe paper or tinted cellophane, tie with gold cord or ribbon and place in mini baskets or small decorative tins.

KIDS

Pat-A-Cake Cookie
& Sprinkle Dip,
page 89

Peanut Butter Cup Cookies

1½ cups firmly packed brown sugar

  1 cup (2 sticks) margarine or butter, softened

 ¾ cup peanut butter (not reduced fat)

  2 eggs

  2 teaspoons vanilla

1½ cups all-purpose flour

 ⅓ cup unsweetened cocoa powder

  1 teaspoon baking soda

 ¼ teaspoon salt (optional)

  2 cups Quaker® Oats (quick or old fashioned, uncooked)

One 9-ounce package miniature peanut butter cup candies, unwrapped, cut into halves or quarters (about 35 candies)

1 Heat oven to 350°F. Beat sugar, margarine and peanut butter until creamy. Add eggs and vanilla; beat well. Add combined flour, cocoa powder, baking soda and salt; mix well. Stir in oats and candy; mix well.

2 Drop dough by level ¼ cupfuls 3 inches apart on ungreased cookie sheets.

3 Bake 12 to 14 minutes or until cookies are slightly firm to the touch. (Do not overbake.) Cool 1 minute on cookie sheets; remove to wire rack. Cool completely. Store tightly covered.

Yield: 3 dozen

DINOSAUR COOKIES

BAKING WITH KIDS

- Schedule baking for early in the day when everyone is well rested.

- Dress kids in comfortable, washable clothes. Roll up sleeves, tie back long hair, wash hands with soap and water and dry with a clean towel.

- Read through the recipe together and give each child a task that's appropriate for his or her age.

- Sit preschoolers at a child-size table and put decorations in nonbreakable bowls. A plastic mat placed beneath the table will simplify cleanup.

²/₃ cup firmly packed brown sugar
½ cup (1 stick) margarine or butter, softened
¼ cup granulated sugar
1 egg
2 tablespoons low-fat milk
1 teaspoon vanilla
¾ cup all-purpose flour
½ teaspoon baking soda
¼ teaspoon salt (optional)
2½ cups Quaker® Oats (quick or old fashioned, uncooked)
2 cups (12 ounces) semisweet chocolate pieces or candy-coated chocolate pieces

Ready-to-spread frosting (optional)
Assorted small candies (optional)

TIP · Younger children will have an easier time shaping dinosaurs if you lightly flour greased cookie sheets. Using your finger, trace the outlines of four large dinosaurs or other kid-pleasing shapes. The kids can then pat the dough inside the lines.

1 Heat oven to 350°F. Lightly grease two cookie sheets.

2 Beat brown sugar, margarine and granulated sugar until creamy. Add egg, milk and vanilla; beat well. Add combined flour, baking soda and salt; mix well. Stir in oats and chocolate pieces; mix well.

3 Divide dough into four equal portions. With moistened hands, pat dough into ¼ inch thick shapes such as dinosaurs or jungle animals on cookie sheets.

4 Bake 12 to 14 minutes or until edges are light golden brown. Cool 2 minutes on cookie sheets; carefully remove to wire rack. Cool completely.

5 Decorate as desired with frosting and candies. Store tightly covered.

Yield: 4 jumbo cookies

1¼ cups all-purpose flour
1 cup Quaker® Oats (quick or old fashioned, uncooked)
½ cup granulated sugar
⅓ cup unsweetened cocoa powder
2 teaspoons baking powder
¼ teaspoon baking soda
⅔ cup mashed ripe bananas (about 2 small)
½ cup skim milk
⅓ cup (5 tablespoons plus 1 teaspoon) margarine, melted
2 egg whites or 1 egg, lightly beaten
1 teaspoon vanilla

Powdered sugar (optional)

TIP· To make standard-size cupcakes, line 12 medium muffin cups with paper baking cups. Proceed as recipe directs. Bake 20 to 25 minutes or until wooden pick inserted in center comes out clean.

1 Heat oven to 400°F. Line 36 miniature muffin cups with paper baking cups or spray bottoms only with no-stick cooking spray.

2 In large bowl, combine flour, oats, granulated sugar, cocoa powder, baking powder and baking soda; mix well. In medium bowl, combine bananas, milk, margarine, egg whites and vanilla; blend well. Add to dry ingredients all at once; stir just until dry ingredients are moistened. (Do not overmix.)

3 Fill muffin cups almost full. Bake 10 to 12 minutes or until wooden pick inserted in center comes out clean. Let cupcakes stand a few minutes; remove from pan. Cool completely on wire rack.

4 Sprinkle with powdered sugar, if desired. Store tightly covered.

Yield: About 3 dozen mini cupcakes

MEASURING HOW-TOS

- Spoon dry ingredients into nested dry measuring cups (plastic or metal) and level with a metal spatula or the straight side of a table knife.

- Thick or sticky ingredients like peanut butter and shortening also should be measured in nested dry measuring cups. Press firmly into cup to eliminate air bubbles and level even with top of cup.

- Measure liquid ingredients in a glass or plastic measuring cup with a spout for pouring. For accuracy, place cup on level surface, pour in liquid and read measure at eye level.

CHOCOLATE COOKIE BEARS

1 cup sugar
½ cup (1 stick) margarine or butter, softened
1 cup (6 ounces) semisweet chocolate pieces, melted
2 eggs
1 teaspoon vanilla
2 cups Quaker® Oats (quick or old fashioned, uncooked)
1½ cups all-purpose flour
1 teaspoon baking powder
¼ teaspoon salt (optional)

Ready-to-spread frosting
Assorted small candies, candy sprinkles, colored sugar

TIP · To melt chocolate: Place in dry glass measuring cup or small bowl. Microwave on HIGH 1 to 2 minutes, stirring every 30 seconds, until smooth. Or, place in top part of double boiler over hot (not boiling) water; stir occasionally until smooth.

1 Beat sugar and margarine until creamy. Add melted chocolate, eggs and vanilla; beat well. Add combined oats, flour, baking powder and salt; mix well. Cover; chill about 2 hours.

2 Heat oven to 350°F. To make bears, shape dough into 1-inch balls for the bodies, ½-inch balls for the heads and ¼-inch balls for the arms, legs and ears. On ungreased cookie sheets, gently press pieces together to form bears, placing 2 inches apart. Flatten bears slightly.

3 Bake 8 to 10 minutes or just until firm to the touch. (Do not overbake.) Cool 2 minutes on cookie sheets; remove to wire rack. Cool completely.

4 Decorate as desired with frosting and candies. Store tightly covered.

Yield: 2 dozen

1 cup (2 sticks) margarine or butter, softened
½ cup sugar
1 teaspoon vanilla
2 cups Quaker® Oats (quick or old fashioned, uncooked)
1¼ cups all-purpose flour
Colored sugar or candy sprinkles

1 Heat oven to 350°F. Place margarine in large (1 gallon) resealable plastic bag; seal. Squeeze with hands until very soft. Open bag; add sugar and vanilla. Reseal; squeeze and knead until ingredients are well mixed. Open bag; add oats and flour. Reseal; squeeze and knead until ingredients are well mixed. Open bag; scrape dough together with spatula and remove from bag.

2 Shape dough into 1-inch balls. Place on ungreased cookie sheets 2 inches apart; flatten with fingers or tines of fork to ¼ inch thickness. Decorate as desired with colored sugar or candy sprinkles.

3 Bake 12 to 14 minutes or until bottoms are light golden brown. Cool 1 minute on cookie sheets; remove to wire rack. Cool completely. Store tightly covered.

Yield: About 3 dozen

SHORTBREAD FUN

Rich and tender shortbread is exceptionally versatile. Try these fun variations.

- Add ¼ cup miniature candy-coated chocolate pieces to dough with the oats and flour.

- Drizzle cooled cookies with melted semisweet chocolate.

- Spread flat side of one cooled cookie with ready-to-spread chocolate frosting; top with flat side of second cookie to make a sandwich. Roll edges in candy sprinkles.

- Arrange several cookies on a dessert plate; top with a scoop of ice cream, chocolate syrup and sliced bananas.

GIANT BROWNIE ICE CREAM SANDWICH

Topping

- ⅓ cup Quaker® Oats (quick or old fashioned, uncooked)
- 3 tablespoons all-purpose flour
- 2 tablespoons firmly packed brown sugar
- ⅓ cup peanut butter (not reduced fat)
- 1 tablespoon margarine or butter

Brownies

- 1 cup (6 ounces) semisweet chocolate pieces
- ½ cup (1 stick) margarine or butter
- ¾ cup granulated sugar
- 1 teaspoon vanilla
- 2 eggs
- 1 cup all-purpose flour
- ¾ cup Quaker® Oats (quick or old fashioned, uncooked)
- ½ teaspoon baking powder
- ¼ teaspoon salt (optional)

- One quart vanilla ice cream or frozen yogurt, softened

1 Heat oven to 350°F. Line two 8 or 9-inch round cake pans with aluminum foil, allowing foil to extend over sides of pans. Spray with no-stick cooking spray or grease lightly.

2 For topping, combine oats, flour and brown sugar. Cut in peanut butter and margarine* with pastry blender or two knives until mixture is crumbly; set aside.

3 For brownies, melt chocolate pieces and margarine in medium saucepan over low heat, stirring frequently. Remove from heat; cool slightly. Stir in sugar and vanilla. Add eggs; mix well. Add combined flour, oats, baking powder and salt; mix well. Divide

batter evenly between pans. Sprinkle with reserved topping, patting gently.

4 Bake 22 to 24 minutes for 8-inch pan (20 to 22 minutes for 9-inch pan) or until center of brownie is set. (Do not overbake.) Cool completely in pans on wire rack.

5 To assemble, spread softened ice cream evenly over one brownie layer while still in pan. Lift second brownie layer out of pan; remove foil. With topping side up, place second brownie layer on top of ice cream, pressing gently. Cover and freeze several hours or overnight.

6 Remove from freezer 10 to 15 minutes before serving. Lift from pan using foil edges. Remove foil; cut into wedges. Store leftovers tightly wrapped in freezer.

Yield: 12 servings

*For an explanation of this technique, see page 37.

Cookies

1	cup (2 sticks) margarine or butter, softened
¾	cup firmly packed brown sugar
1	tablespoon water
1	teaspoon vanilla
2	cups Quaker® Oats (quick or old fashioned, uncooked)
1¼	cups all-purpose flour
1	teaspoon ground cinnamon
½	teaspoon baking soda
¼	teaspoon salt (optional)

Dip

One	8-ounce container frozen whipped topping, thawed
¼	cup multicolored candy sprinkles

TIP· For individual cookies, drop dough by teaspoonfuls 2 inches apart on lightly greased cookie sheets. With lightly floured hands, flatten about ⅛ inch thick. Bake 6 to 8 minutes or until light golden brown. Cool on wire rack. Makes about 3 dozen.

1 Heat oven to 375°F. Lightly grease two large cookie sheets.

2 Beat margarine and sugar until creamy. Add water and vanilla; beat well. Add combined oats, flour, cinnamon, baking soda and salt; mix well.

3 Spoon half of dough onto one cookie sheet. With lightly floured hands, pat into a 10 x 12-inch rectangle about ⅛ inch thick. Repeat with remaining dough and second cookie sheet.

4 Bake 8 to 11 minutes or until edges are golden brown, rotating cookie sheets* after 5 minutes. Immediately cut each rectangle into 24 pieces. Remove pieces to wire rack; cool completely.

5 Combine whipped topping and sprinkles; mix well. Serve dip with cookies. Store cookies tightly covered. Refrigerate leftover dip.

Yield: 4 dozen

*For an explanation of this technique, see page 17.

1995 First Prize—Just for Kids
Rosemarie Berger and Callie Moore, Jamestown, N

1 cup (6 ounces) semisweet chocolate pieces
1 cup (6 ounces) butterscotch pieces
1½ cups Quaker® Oats (quick or old fashioned, uncooked)
1 cup chopped peanuts

1 Line bottom of 13 x 9-inch baking pan with waxed paper.

2 Place chocolate and butterscotch pieces in microwaveable bowl. Microwave on HIGH 30 seconds to 1½ minutes or until mixture is melted and smooth, stirring every 30 seconds. Add oats and peanuts; mix well.

3 Drop by heaping teaspoonfuls onto waxed paper-lined pan. Chill until firm. Store tightly covered in refrigerator.

Yield: 3 dozen

NO-BAKE FUDGE CLUSTERS

2 cups sugar
½ cup (1 stick) margarine or butter
½ cup low-fat milk
⅓ cup unsweetened cocoa powder
3 cups Quaker® Oats (quick or old fashioned, uncooked)

1 Line cookie sheets with waxed paper or spray with no-stick cooking spray.

2 In large saucepan, combine sugar, margarine, milk and cocoa powder. Bring to a boil over medium heat, stirring frequently. Continue boiling 3 minutes, stirring frequently.

3 Remove from heat. Add oats; mix well.* Drop by tablespoonfuls onto cookie sheets. Let stand until firm. Store tightly covered at room temperature.

*If using old fashioned oats, cool mixture in saucepan 5 minutes.

Yield: About 3 dozen

EQUIVALENTS

3 teaspoons = 1 tablespoon
4 tablespoons = ¼ cup
5 tablespoons + 1 teaspoon = ⅓ cup
8 tablespoons = ½ cup
10 tablespoons + 2 teaspoons = ⅔ cup
12 tablespoons = ¾ cup
16 tablespoons = 1 cup

- TIP: When measuring margarine or butter, use the markings on the wrapper as your guide.

¼ cup = ½ stick = 4 tablespoons
½ cup = 1 stick = 8 tablespoons
¾ cup = 1½ sticks = 12 tablespoons
1 cup = 2 sticks = ½ pound
2 cups = 4 sticks = 1 pound

This chocolatey, no-bake oatmeal cookie recipe was created in the early 1960s. Also known as 3-Minute Cookies, it continues to be one of our most requested recipes.

		page	calories	calories from fat	total fat (g)	saturated fat (g)	cholesterol (mg)	sodium (mg)	protein (g)	dietary fiber (g)
Apple Oatmeal Spice Cookies	1 cookie	11	90	15	1.5	0	0	45	2	<1
Applesauce Oatmeal Muffins	1 muffin	27	180	40	5	0.5	0	110	4	2
Baked Breakfast Oatmeal	1/8 of recipe	70	260	30	3.5	0.5	0	90	9	3 (1g soluble fiber)
Banana Oatmeal Rocks	1 cookie	13	130	50	6	0.5	<5	60	1	1
Blueberry Streusel Bars	1 bar	21	190	80	9	1.5	0	105	2	1
California Lemon Crunch Dessert	1/15 of recipe	55	330	190	21	8	0	200	4	2
Caramel Oatmeal Chewies	1 bar	22	180	80	9	2.5	0	85	2	1
Cherry Nectarine Crisps	1 crisp	44	210	60	7	1	0	70	3	3
Chewy Choc-Oat-Chip™ Cookies	1 cookie	10	100	50	5	2	5	55	1	<1
Chocolate Cookie Bears	1 undecorated cookie	86	160	60	7	2.5	15	60	3	1
Chocolate Raspberry Squares	1 square	23	120	50	6	1.5	0	50	1	<1
Citrus Streusel Squares	1 square	78	210	70	8	2	5	115	3	<1
Cocoa Banana Mini Cakes	1 mini cupcake	85	60	20	2	0	0	55	1	<1
Cocoa Oatmeal Cookies	1 cookie	16	100	40	4.5	0.5	10	75	2	<1
Cranberry Orange Bread	1/12 of loaf	33	240	70	8	1.5	55	95	5	2
Cuban Meatball Kabobs	1/6 of recipe	61	260	100	11	4	45	140	16	3
Dilled Salmon Cakes	1/5 of recipe	62	180	55	6	1	30	400	19	2
Dinosaur Cookies	1/12 of recipe	84	370	170	19	7	20	150	5	4
Double Berry Cake	1/12 of cake	48	320	110	12	2.5	<5	250	5	2
Easy Apple Custard Pie	1/8 of pie	50	490	190	21	5	60	250	7	3
Easy Shortbread Cookies	1 cookie	87	90	50	5	1	0	60	1	<1
Famous Oatmeal Cookies	1 cookie	12	70	25	3	0.5	<5	10	1	0
Favorite Oatmeal Pancakes	3 pancakes	72	260	50	6	1	55	200	10	2
Festive Eggnog Bread	1/12 of loaf	36	300	80	9	2	50	95	5	2

< = less than

		page	calories	calories from fat	total fat (g)	saturated fat (g)	cholesterol (mg)	sodium (mg)	protein (g)	dietary fiber (g)
Fresh Fruit Crisp	⅑ of recipe	43	170	50	6	1	0	65	2	2
Frosted Pumpkin Softies	1 cookie	79	130	45	5	1	5	75	1	<1
Fruit & Honey Granola	½ cup	67	230	50	6	1	0	70	5	3 (1g soluble fiber)
Garden Pizzas	1 pizza	63	430	130	14	6	25	340	22	4
Garden-Style Turkey Loaf	⅛ of recipe	57	150	20	2	0.5	40	105	24	3
Giant Brownie Ice Cream Sandwich	1/12 of recipe	88	420	210	23	8	55	200	7	2
Ginger Oat Crumb Cake	1/12 of cake	47	340	80	8	1.5	0	200	4	2
Go Bananas Cookie Sundaes	1 cookie w/o topping	74	230	100	11	3	15	140	3	2
Holiday Cookie Surprises	1 cookie	80	80	35	4	0.5	<5	45	1	0
Honey Lime Oat Muffins	1 muffin	29	190	30	3	0.5	0	100	4	1
Italian Herbed Oatmeal Focaccia	1/12 of bread	40	180	70	8	1.5	0	190	4	2
Lazy Daisy Oatmeal Cake	1/12 of cake	46	360	80	9	2.5	0	220	4	2
Lemon Blueberry Oatmeal Muffins	1 muffin	26	160	30	3	0	0	110	4	2
Lemon Poppy Seed Cake	1/16 of cake	45	280	100	11	2.5	40	230	5	2
Lemon Wafers	1 cookie	18	70	20	2	0	0	45	1	0
Maple Apple Oatmeal	¼ of recipe	69	300	25	3	0.5	0	30	7	5 (2g soluble fiber)
Mini Tex-Mex Meatloaves	⅙ of recipe	60	340	190	21	9	120	280	26	2
Mocha Chip Cheesecake Bars	1 bar	54	260	150	17	9	60	140	5	1
No-Bake Chocolate Scotchies	1 cookie	90	90	45	5	2.5	0	40	2	<1
No-Bake Fudge Clusters	1 cookie	91	100	30	3	0.5	0	35	1	1
Not-So-Sinful Sundae Pie	⅛ of pie	52	280	80	9	1.5	0	140	4	2
Oatmeal Butter Brittle Cookies	1 cookie piece	17	130	70	8	4	10	45	2	1
Oatmeal Carrot Cake Bread	1/16 of loaf	34	210	35	4	0.5	0	125	4	2
Oatmeal Dream Dates	1 bar	24	210	100	11	2.5	0	95	2	2

< = less than

		page	calories	calories from fat	total fat (g)	saturated fat (g)	cholesterol (mg)	sodium (mg)	protein (g)	dietary fiber (g)
Oatmeal Macaroons	1 cookie	14	90	45	5	1.5	10	70	1	<1
Oatmeal Scotchies	1 cookie	15	140	60	7	3.5	10	80	2	<1
Oat Pecan Praline Cookies	1 cookie	19	120	60	7	1	10	70	2	<1
Old Fashioned Oatmeal Pie	1/10 of pie	49	320	110	13	4.5	50	180	4	<1
Orange Banana Date Oatmeal	1/4 of recipe	71	290	20	2	0	0	5	7	6 (2g soluble fiber)
Pat-A-Cake Cookies	1 cookie w/ 1Tbsp. dip	89	90	45	5	1.5	0	60	1	0
Peach Muesli With Berries	1 cup w/ 1/3 cup berries	68	300	35	3.5	1	<5	45	10	7 (3g soluble fiber)
Peanut Butter Cup Cookies	1 cookie	83	190	100	11	3.5	10	150	4	2
Peanutty Crisscrosses	1 cookie	20	70	30	3	0.5	<5	40	1	<1
Pear Ginger Scones	1 scone	37	150	40	4	0.5	0	160	4	1
Plum Almond Muffins	1 muffin	30	180	45	5	1	0	115	4	2
Prize-Winning Meatloaf	1/8 of recipe	59	210	110	12	4.5	80	160	17	1
Pumpkin Silk Pie	1/10 of pie	53	390	180	20	8	15	370	8	3
Quaker's Best Oatmeal Bread	1/16 of loaf	39	130	20	2	0	0	210	4	1
Quaker's Best Oatmeal Cookies	1 cookie	9	130	60	7	1.5	5	110	2	<1
Quaker's Best Oatmeal Muffins	1 muffin	31	240	80	9	2	20	170	5	1
Really Big Birthday Cookie	1/12 undecorated cookie	75	170	80	9	1.5	15	120	3	1
Scottish Oat Scones	1 scone	38	220	90	11	2	20	220	4	2
Spring-Into-Easter Cutouts	1 undecorated cookie	77	80	35	4	0.5	<5	70	1	0
Sunday Supper Meatloaf	1/6 of recipe	58	470	190	21	7	105	440	26	6
Valentine Cookie Puzzle	2 undecorated pieces	76	200	110	12	2	0	135	3	1
Whole Grain Banana Muffins	1 muffin	28	190	50	6	1	0	210	4	1

< = less than

INDEX